Praise for (

Can we really "speak the truth in love"? Chaplain Charles Causey answers "yes." In fact, he believes it is the only way to have authentic friendships and become authentic leaders. His twenty-two strategies for overcoming fear and learning to lovingly speak with candor give practical help for all who aspire to genuinely help others.

GARY D. CHAPMAN
Author of *The 5 Love Languages*

Candor is a solid work, providing the weight needed to create significant changes in our lives. By identifying the keys to true candor, along with suggestions for giving and receiving honest feedback, Causey gives us the tools to help us grow in our relationships at work, with our family, ourselves, and our friends.

PAUL WHITE
President, *Appreciation at Work*

Candor is arriving on the stage of America's public and private discourse at just the right time. This book will enable communication with both truth and love, moving beyond our prevalent spirit of sensitivity to achieve true understanding and respect for others. A must-read!

ROBERT F. DEES
Major General, US Army, retired
President, National Center for Healthy Veterans

Truth matters. Character matters. Love conquers fear. *Candor* by Charles Causey delivers on the promise of conversing with integrity and honesty.

CYNTHIA BRIAN
New York Times bestselling author; TV/Radio personality; founder, Be the Star You Are!

In Charles Causey's latest book, you will not only increase your confidence to say what's truly on your mind rather than what others want to hear, but you will learn to do it with character and compassion. This is the book I wish had existed back when I was in school. It is a wise, formational, and deeply nuanced work that will help you increase trust and deepen your most important relationships.

KEN WYTSMA
Award-winning author of *The Myth of Equality* and *Redeeming How We Talk*

In Causey's latest writing, he unpacks a societal truth that can no longer be ignored. Candor, or being forthright, honest, and sincere, is a social skill that needs to be sharpened for us to grow in relationships and community. If recent years have taught us anything, it is that too many people don't know how to speak the truth in love. This will help and is much-needed writing for this time in history!

TONY MILTENBERGER
Lead Pastor, Restoration Church, Centerville, OH, and host of the *Reclamation Podcast*

I agree with Charles that candor—being honest, open, and straightforward in our conversations—needs to be reintroduced into our thinking. *Candor* will offer *you* a great opportunity to be exposed to twenty-two strategies that can help you overcome the fear of offending when all you want to do is speak the truth in love!

JIM GEORGE
Author of the bestselling book *A Man After God's Own Heart*

GABRIEL DUMAX
PUBLIC LIBRARY

Caring, transparent communication is evaporating from our society as we have become engulfed by an ever-increasingly polarized world, with the trend now overtaking organizations, churches, and even families. This book gets to the root of the problem and offers transformational solutions.

ROGER PARROTT
President, Belhaven University

Charles Causey has given our modern-day society a gift in this book. With social media granting everyone and their brother full access to free expression, rancor has replaced candor. This book, with winsome words, stories from day-to-day living, and very practical exercises, is a timely resource for every arena—family life, community, church, and business. The reflection questions and candor commitments will challenge you, the reader, to put into practice the tenets of this book. Read this book slowly, then candidly embrace its principles by living them out!

DON PAPE
Curator, Pape Commons, and former publisher

If you're satisfied with mediocrity in communication with your family, friends, and coworkers, feel free to skip this book. But if you want to rocket those relationships to new heights of connection and trust, dive into Charles Causey's practical wisdom in his newest book, *Candor*. Truth-saturated and highly accessible, you will be encouraged (and stretched!) to "speak the truth in love" in ways that actually build and transform yourself and others. Causey avoids the common conversation extremes of brutal honesty or terminal niceness. Instead, he skillfully guides us on a path of communicating with greater openness and understanding. *Candor* will help repair troubled relationships . . . and make good ones even healthier. I highly recommend this breath-of-fresh-air book!

QUINTIN STIEFF
Lead Pastor, Valley Church, West Des Moines, IA

As a woman with extensive ministry experience in a milieu dominated by men, I can tell you that my lack of candor has frequently been driven by a deep concern over being punished. In *Candor*, Charles Causey has provided a vital resource for those needing to speak truth in environments that might not welcome candor, and a timely tool for leaders at all levels who need to actively seek and thoughtfully listen to feedback from others.

GRETCHEN KNUDSON GEE
Principal Lecturer, President's Distinguished Teaching Fellow, Northern Arizona University

In *Candor*, Charles gives concrete ways to make this verse extremely applicable to our everyday lives. As we've made our way as a married couple, we've learned these principles do work, at times learning the hard way. I guarantee that as you read this book, you will think of occasions in the past you will wish you could do over, and you will consider current situations where you can apply these truths.

LAURI CAUSEY
Wife of author and witness to these truths applied

Candor

The Secret to Succeeding at Tough Conversations

Charles Causey

NORTHFIELD PUBLISHING

CHICAGO

© 2021 by
CHARLES CAUSEY

All rights reserved. No part of this book may be reproduced in any form without permission in writing from the publisher, except in the case of brief quotations embodied in critical articles or reviews.

Unless indicated otherwise, Scripture quotations are taken from the (NASB®) New American Standard Bible®, Copyright © 1960, 1971, 1977, 1995 by The Lockman Foundation. Used by permission. All rights reserved. www.lockman.org.). Copyright © 1960, 1971, 1977, 1995 by The Lockman Foundation. Used by permission. www.Lockman.org

Scripture quotations marked (NIV) are taken from the Holy Bible, New International Version®, NIV®. Copyright © 1973, 1978, 1984, 2011 by Biblica, Inc.™ Used by permission of Zondervan. All rights reserved worldwide. www.zondervan.com The "NIV" and "New International Version" are trademarks registered in the United States Patent and Trademark Office by Biblica, Inc.™

Scripture quotations marked (BSB) are taken from The Holy Bible, Berean Study Bible, BSB. Copyright © 2016, 2018 by Bible Hub. Used by permission. All rights reserved worldwide.

All emphasis in Scripture has been added.

Names and details of some stories have been changed to protect the privacy of individuals.

Published in association with The Steve Laube Agency.

Edited by Amanda Cleary Eastep
Interior Design: Puckett Smartt
Cover Design: Charles Brock

All websites and phone numbers listed herein are accurate at the time of publication but may change in the future or cease to exist. The listing of website references and resources does not imply publisher endorsement of the site's entire contents. Groups and organizations are listed for informational purposes, and listing does not imply publisher endorsement of their activities.

Library of Congress Cataloging-in-Publication Data

Names: Causey, Charles, author.
Title: Candor : the secret to succeeding at tough conversations / Charles Causey.
Description: Chicago : Northfield Publishing, [2021] | Includes bibliographical references. | Summary: "In a society where sensitivities take precedence over truth, it can often feel impossible to openly speak your mind. In Candor, you'll learn how truth and love together can unlock pathways to more effective leadership and relationships-even in a day and age when many remain silent for fear of speaking up"-- Provided by publisher.
Identifiers: LCCN 2020047117 (print) | LCCN 2020047118 (ebook) | ISBN 9780802420770 (paperback) | ISBN 9780802499066 (ebook)
Subjects: LCSH: Interpersonal communication--Religious aspects--Christianity. | Communication in organizations--Religious aspects--Christianity. | Conversations--Religious aspects--Christianity | Honesty--Religious aspects--Christianity. | Sincerity--Religious aspects--Christianity. | Leadership--Religious aspects--Christianity.
Classification: LCC BV4597.53.C64 C38 2021 (print) | LCC BV4597.53.C64 (ebook) | DDC 248.4--dc23
LC record available at https://lccn.loc.gov/2020047117
LC ebook record available at https://lccn.loc.gov/2020047118

We hope you enjoy this book from Northfield Publishing. Our goal is to provide high-quality, thought-provoking books and products that connect truth to your real needs and challenges. For more information on other books and products that will help you with all your important relationships, go to northfieldpublishing.com or write to:

Northfield Publishing
820 N. LaSalle Boulevard
Chicago, IL 60610

1 3 5 7 9 10 8 6 4 2

Printed in the United States of America

for
Madison and Hannah

Contents

The EMPEROR HAS NO CLOTHES

Many of us have remained silent far too long.

Poor decisions are made every day because good people with honest intentions find it hard to take action and make a stand. Instead, they suffer under intense internal pressure *not* to speak up. Others have stepped out and tried candor only to be punished for it.

As an example, several times during her esteemed career, political science professor Gretchen Gee spoke up regarding an issue she strongly felt the organization needed to address only to be later reprimanded. "I was called in by a leader and told that I was wrong to speak up," Gretchen recalled. "I was talked about as having 'lost credibility,' and I was even obliquely threatened with removal from the program I was leading."[1]

When people are routinely rewarded for quiet compliance and criticized for going against the flow, is it any wonder that candor is desperately lacking? It may be easier, in some respects, not to speak up about issues that concern us. It allows meetings to continue without disruption. It keeps the peace. It avoids unwanted attention. However, it does not benefit an organization at its deepest level—

> • • •
>
> **Family dynamics can be improved, friendships can grow, and organizations can thrive by growing in the critical area of candor.**
>
> • • •

that of forming a bedrock of trust among its members.

Today, the perception may be that there is too much candor in our culture, especially on social media and in politics; but this is not the type of candor we're talking about. The kind of candor as defined in this book is desperately needed and becomes a passageway in our society for greater intimacy and trust with all of our most important relationships. Family dynamics can be improved, friendships can grow, and organizations—from start-ups to behemoth tech companies—can thrive by growing in the critical area of candor.

Thankfully, some companies have not been afraid of open dialogue. Take, for instance, this well-known story from Motorola in the 1980s.

A young middle manager . . . approached then-CEO Robert Galvin and said: "Bob, I heard that point you made this morning, and I think you're dead wrong. I'm going to prove it: *I'm going to shoot you down.*" When the young man stormed off, Galvin, beaming proudly, turned to a companion and said, "That's how we've overcome Texas Instruments' lead in semiconductors!"[2]

Companies tend to thrive when they reward candor instead of punishing it.

The former chairman and CEO of General Electric, Jack Welch, has long held that institutions suffer because of a lack of candor. He went on several speaking tours and mentorship engagements with corporations exclaiming the need for it. He said that the biggest dirty little secret in business is the lack of candor in every culture, country, society, and social class.[3]

Candor is essential regardless of the business size or mission. My sister Carol explained to me that as a college student working in a grocery store, she noticed that high school employees were allowing their friends to slip candy bars and snacks through the line without paying for them. Carol courageously stepped out, risking the relationships of those with whom she worked. When she confronted the manager about it, he did not believe her; apparently, he *just knew* they were good kids. A few weeks later, an assistant manager told Carol that the manager realized my sister was right. He had installed cameras and discovered the high schoolers letting their friends pilfer the store. In a small way, Carol's candor made a difference to the bottom line.

Candor is not only needed in business, but in our government, our schools, our military, our churches, our marriages, and our prayer times. Lives without candor can lead to hypocrisy, bitterness, lying, gossip, and downright division. Lives with candor are more interesting, expectant, truthful, and exploratory.

Candor helps us build relationships because it requires us to be courageous, vulnerable, and willing to offer feedback. It leverages openness and honesty to increase trust. It brings greater value to organizations and relationships.

Sitting in an in-person meeting with a screen-saver face on may seem expedient in the moment, but a deficiency of candor impedes communication channels and eventually erodes confidence and trust. Understanding the forces supporting and constraining candor is essential and is the purpose of this book.

Is there a general reluctance to speak with candor? I conducted a simple survey of five hundred people. Participants were to complete the statement: "When I hear something that does not sound quite accurate, I . . ." with one of two options:

1. Look for an opportunity to approach the matter diplomatically.
2. Immediately correct the person speaking.

Of respondents, 80.2 percent chose the "diplomatic" answer, and 19.8 percent chose the "immediately correct" option. Four out of five people stated a reluctance to speak up when they heard something inaccurate. This data was taken from random people across the country over a period of two years in conjunction with a battery of other questions. The results offer a snapshot of the hesitation at the root of our day-to-day interactions with others.

The main reasons we refrain from speaking often are not introversion, shyness, or not knowing what to say. Something lies deeper at the core of who we are, and it affects our confidence. Many of us live in fear of our future, of hurting others, or of having our truest feelings exposed. *What if someone sees the real me?*

Yes, speaking with candor always involves authenticity and often risk, but wouldn't it be better to present the naked truth instead of spending a life exchanging nervous pleasantries? A resurgence of candor in society is desperately needed today to create authentic, close relationships. This book was written to give people effective strategies in overcoming fear and developing candor.

Mark has worked for a Fortune 1000 company for fifteen years. After several promotions, he feels the company has become a good fit, and he hopes to retire from there. However, he explained that he routinely attends meetings where poor decisions are made because people fail to speak up. Many times a work associate will whisper to him after a meeting, "Well, that was a dumb decision the leaders made in there," to which Mark responds, "Then why didn't you say anything?" He said the typical answer is that the employee did not think it would make a difference and instead cause waves for no reason. Mark ponders how much more effective the organization could be if people truly spoke their mind.

* * *

What exactly is candor? Remember the old story, "The Emperor's New Clothes"?[4] Here is a quick summary: Once there was an emperor who was so exceedingly in love with new clothes that he spent all his money on being well dressed. One day, two swindlers came to town guaranteeing that the cloth they used was so magical, it was invisible to anyone not qualified for office or for those unusually stupid. *Those would be just the clothes for me,* thought the emperor. *If I wore them, I could tell the wise men from the fools.* Once the garments were ready, the emperor showed them off in a special parade. All the onlookers, having heard the claim of the weavers, praised the emperor's apparel. "Oh, how fine are the emperor's new clothes! Don't they fit him to perfection? And see his long train!" Nobody would confess that they couldn't see any clothes at all, except for one young boy in the crowd, who stood and watched with wrinkled brow. "But he hasn't got anything on." The emperor shivered, for he suspected the boy was right. But he thought, *The procession must go on!* So he walked with his head high and as proudly as ever, with his noblemen trailing behind, holding high the train that wasn't there.

The story of the emperor's new clothes retains its appeal because of its perennial audit on contemporary society. The weavers are those who fool others with human cunning, craftiness, and deceitful scheming. The emperor might be an organizational leader who is only interested in hearing positive things about his or her leadership. The emperor's noblemen are those sycophants who will say anything to stay in their position and keep their leader happy. The young boy is the person who is honest and courageous enough to tell the truth. There was no incentive for the child to lie; he didn't know or care about what the emperor thought.

The entire town, including the emperor, hopefully learned something valuable that day about pride and the desire to please leaders with words. Many thought there would be repercussions if they were honest. It took childish innocence to declare the truth—that the emperor was unrobed and walking down the road as naked as the day he was born. That day, the king became a child, and the child became a king.

This folktale shows the significance of candor in our everyday lives. Candor is the quality of being forthright, honest, and sincere. It can be a highly effective tool to shape our spheres of influence.

How does it work? Candor sheds light on a situation, allowing important issues to be discovered. As a surgeon needs good light to see the operation he may be performing, important discussions need candor to find the truth. Without it, there is doubt, disengagement, and confusion, as we try to decipher what people's words really mean. With candor, meetings are expedited and projects can move forward. Candor will not only help the organizations we serve, it will sharpen us as individuals. If we allow others to be candid with us—and in the process become conduits for receiving feedback—it will take us to places of trust and loyalty we never thought possible.

Candor is the quality of being forthright, honest, and sincere.

I am writing this book in the midst of a military career. I've had commanders who told me that I owe them candor, as if it were a debt I could pay only by being forthright and honest. Speaking with candor is definitely a type of obligation, not only in the military, but in politics, government work, and other institutions. In 2018, a high-ranking FBI agent, Andrew McCabe, was fired just days before his retirement for a lack of candor in his answers to investigators. Immediately following the incident, internet searches for the word "candor" increased 5,600 percent.[5] Candor is also necessary in churches. I served in full-time ministry for twelve years before entering active duty, and I have witnessed how candor can positively impact church ministry with its complex network of relationships.

What's interesting is that many people in churches and busi-nesses run from candor, fearing that it will create unnecessary dis-comfort in relationships. However, when candor is embraced by caring people, it engenders a renewed sense of hope and strength in our important relationships. What's more, if I practice candor in my personal life, it can improve my marriage, my relationship to my children, and my faith. Using candor in prayer is not just a type of therapy, it whittles deeply into the layers of my own self-awareness and core beliefs of an all-powerful and loving God.

As we grow up, we learn from our families about what to notice, and what to say about what we notice. But we also learn something else—what *not* to say about what we notice. For instance, if Mom and Dad are routinely in conflict at the supper table or when driv-ing from place to place, their conflict simply becomes something *peculiar to the family* dynamic; children learn to never speak openly about it. This type of learning about what not to speak about, or learned avoidance, carries into our adult lives. When a boss is be-ing rude or mean for no apparent reason, we tend to put the action in our *peculiar to the organization* file and can simply refuse to ac-knowledge it. *That's just him*, we might decide, to the detriment of everyone around us.

However, people in authority need those they lead to speak up about what they are seeing. Doing so will create a deeper sense of belonging and trust when subordinates are allowed to challenge the status quo and speak the unspoken truth. Leaders have to be self-aware and confident in order to allow this type of openness and re-ceive feedback. It takes a strong leader to not only receive feedback, but also integrate it into the organizational dynamic for greater gain. Such leaders do not have to be the smartest ones in the room, and they are not ruled by what others think of them. They desire for the entire organization to succeed, so they anchor all their relationships in a sea of trust where candid feedback is rewarded. When the tide comes in, all boats are lifted.

My goal in writing this book is for the reader to learn to overcome personal fears and cynicism when speaking and to develop skills in wielding candor so that it becomes habitual and others-centered. My goal is also for leaders to learn to be willing to hear things they don't like without feeling threatened, lashing out, and punishing well-intentioned honesty.

Readers will learn to mitigate the #1 enemy of candor that zaps honesty and forthrightness out of any well-meaning interaction, understand the fundamentals of ancient candor, and practice utilizing candor in all of his or her most important relationships. Finally, it is my hope that every reader will integrate the Candor Commitments found at the end of each chapter and utilize the 22 Strategies for Effective Candor to help their organizations build deeper trust.

Don't be content in the relationship shallows; it is magnificently more rewarding when we speak up and encourage others by not only telling them the truth, but allowing them to tell the truth to us as well.

CHAPTER 1

SPEAK the UNSPOKEN TRUTH

Speaking the truth in love . . .[1]

"I have a concern."

My statement rang in the air for a moment, stopping the meeting.

For years, other board members had allowed the chairman to bully his way on every decision. I was new to the trade. It was my first real job on the East Coast and in this industry. I had never dealt with this type of particular board makeup, and I felt a little out of my league. Certainly, one of the longtime board members would stand up to the man, but they remained silent. It was down to the wire. We were approving the list of nominees for next year's board members. His name was at the top of the list. He could easily slide back into his role as chairman of the board. In that influential position, he would delay any progress over the next three years.

"Out with it, young buck!" the chairman bellowed. He was a little perturbed that I was slowing the progress of the meeting. He had no idea that my concern was about him, and that I was about to bring up something that would disrupt the meeting and jeopardize his leadership.

Prior to the meeting, I had memorized a verse from the Bible in the book of Job: "I am young in years and you are old; therefore I was shy and afraid to tell you what I think. I thought age should speak, and increased years should teach wisdom. But it is a spirit in man, and the breath of the Almighty gives them understanding. The abundant in years may not be wise."[2] These words gave me confidence, along with the deep impression that it was up to me to help shed light on a dark situation. The emperor had no clothes, and I was the only one willing to speak up.

"Jim, my concern is with one of the names on the ballot."

"Whose name?"

"Yours."

It was a record-scratch moment bringing cosmic discomfort. Most of the other board members looked down at their notes and fidgeted while I stated my case. They knew that what I was bringing out into the open needed to be addressed, but everyone was scared of confrontation. This meekness and passivity led to a blatant disregard for procedure during the chairman's tenure. For instance, the chairman and another board member would make decisions on some of the agenda items before the meeting in order to avoid unwanted discussion. But this was not my greatest frustration.

The way in which he dealt with board decisions outside of the boardroom caused division. If a decision did not go his way during a board meeting, his negative reaction to it in the public realm caused disunity across the wider organization, requiring the issue to be addressed again. It seemed he purposely wanted to stir up muck to make it tough on the other leaders. Interestingly, the chairman sat quietly and listened to all I had to say. It was actually another member of the board, his friend, who jumped to his feet during the discussion and made several unfounded accusations, uncannily against other members of the board, not I. Then he fled the twelve-story building. This rattled everyone and emotions were high. The chairman eventually stood up, stated that his intentions had always been honorable, and departed. The rest of us sat there looking at each other. Two were now gone and five were left. And those remaining at the table did not look very happy with me.

What had just happened? How had it come to this?

At first glance, it could appear that I not only ruined the meeting, but I nearly caused the board and the organization it represented to split. I was scolded in private by a third member of the board. He was trying to be a friend to me but explained that I could have gone about things a little more diplomatically. In my opinion, all of the issues I was concerned about were publicly displayed, so I felt they needed to be addressed publicly. But I questioned myself: perhaps there was a better option than the one I chose.

I didn't sleep well for days. I had no appetite. In fact, I had a horrible feeling in the pit of my stomach. It was the Christmas season, and I was not in a festive nor spiritually reflective mood.

My speaking up appeared to be a failure. It did not bring unity; it brought temporary disunity. We had to invite a third-party moderator from another organization to work with the board in order for there to be civil discourse and move forward. This was painfully humbling for me.

To make matters worse, the moderator found out it was my birthday, and he made everyone in the room sing "Happy Birthday" to me. Some grimaced through the forced rendition of the usually festive tune. That was a low point for me. Over time, however, I was able to see how speaking up changed not only the board makeup, but the organization and the customers we served.

After deliberating all the issues with the moderator, both the chairman and his friend voluntarily decided not to run again. This allowed us to bring in other well-qualified people to serve on the board and to have a new chairman. Soon, the health of the entire organization drastically improved.

There was a unity and peace among the board members that I had never experienced during the few years I had been serving. We held the first vision retreat for this organization in a decade. Underlying issues were openly brought up and discussed, no longer allowed to fester underneath the surface of conversations causing discord and frustration. The leaders actually looked forward to meetings instead of dreading them. We did not have to guess at what someone was really thinking.

Up until then, meetings had been held in the evenings and were supposed to max out at two hours. However, because of a lack of trust and poor management, the meetings sometimes took four or five hours and were exhausting. Under fresh leadership, the meetings ended much sooner. There was noticeably more agreement than disagreement. Members no longer feared retribution, so they spoke the truth and didn't waste time trying to decipher what people really meant. Candor and trust sped up the meeting process, and ending on time made entire families happier. Board members could now tuck their children into bed when they arrived home.

I also discovered that I had personally grown through the challenge. It was a groundbreaking, character-enhancing moment in my life. I had changed as a result of speaking up. Though for a few days I hated the feelings I experienced after the incident, I did not hate the results. If anything, I had waited too long to have candor. Not speaking up sooner was my sole regret with the entire experience. And, I did eventually visit the two board members at their homes in order to communicate my care and to restore trust.

CANDOR VS. CAMOUFLAGE

I've often thought about that meeting and wondered what might have been the result if I hadn't spoken up. I was battling intense emotions during the hour leading up to my statements about the chairman. I knew that certain issues needed to be addressed about his leadership, but I wasn't sure I was the right person to do it. It seemed entirely reasonable to me to wait it out, hoping that someone else would speak up. In fact, I *had* waited it out for several agonizing board meetings, but no one ever spoke up.

The opposite of candor is camouflage, a disguise to cover over the truth instead of exposing it. We use camouflage in the military so we can hide things from the enemy, diverting attention away from what is really there. We use camouflage netting to cover vehicles, antiaircraft guns, and even generators. The goal is to disguise *everything*. Our tents are green in woodland and tropical environments to blend in with the forest and grass; our vehicles are painted, our uniforms are camouflage, and our face is painted when we run exercises. The goal is to be invisible.

As I sat through multiple meetings, stone silent instead of speaking up about issues, I was camouflaging my true thoughts and emotions. This happens when we don't trust others. Many of us are experts at being invisible. We share a reluctance to speak with candor and prefer camouflage, but candor is necessary. Candor may not only change meetings; it might change entire organizations.

So, what exactly does the word candor mean?

The Latin root of the English word candor is *candēre,* and it means brilliant whiteness, "to shine or glow."[3] ("Candle" is derived from it.) The word candor describes something that sheds light on a situation. It means to demonstrate a straightforwardness, sincerity, openness, truthfulness, and frankness. In its simplest form, the two words best used to describe candor to others are forthright honesty. This is the opposite of camouflage.

While it may not be viewed this way today, candor is also defined as a form of kindness; to speak to someone with candor was to give them a gift.[4] It was actually considered loving to speak the truth to others. Some have also taken it to mean bluntness, and others rudeness, but this takes its definition farther than is justified.

Another aspect of speaking with candor is being prepared to own the truths we are speaking. I'm responsible for the truth I am offering right now. I've got to own it. I was told long ago that there are very few "just kiddings," meaning that sometimes candor is passed off as a joke to ease the pain it might inflict on the recipient. We have to be responsible for the truths we share and not camouflage them with the words "just kidding."

As important as knowing what candor is, it is also important to know what candor is not.

THE MYTHS OF CANDOR

Candor does not involve being critical, attacking someone else, or demonizing a person to others. If communicated rightly, you won't offend the person you're talking to. In fact, if you do, you have probably not demonstrated true candor.

To understand what true candor is, let's look at what it isn't. Consider these five myths:

1. You have to be an extrovert to communicate candidly.

Actually, often introverts display true candor more than extroverts because they have internally processed items and deliberately speak truth when the time calls for it. Appropriately speaking up is a sign of emotional maturity, not extroversion.

2. Candor is being brash or rude.

Candor can be delivered in a loving manner.

3. You risk your career when you speak with candor.

In some situations, this may be accurate, such as in toxic environments fueled by narcissistic leaders (see chapters 7 and 8). In many organizations—at least healthy ones—supervisors increase respect for employees when they see they are not too afraid to contribute constructively. General George C. Marshall courageously used candor in World War I with General John J. Pershing, and again in World War II with President Franklin D. Roosevelt, both times with great results for him and for the country.

4. Candor is all about criticism and being negative.

Although it may sometimes express disagreement, it is most helpful when it brings something positive to the discussion.

5. Candor should only be used rarely.

On the contrary, the more candor the better. It infuses honesty into conversations, so it should flow freely. Speak the unspoken truth and reap the results.

Now that we have looked at what is not factual, we can look at what is actually true about candor.

THE ESSENCE OF CANDOR

What is the essence of true candor? Candor is a gift to others. It means having the courage to speak up when it is necessary. It is about being authentic and honest with others about your true feelings and appropriately disclosing information about yourself or others for the good of those who hear. Having candor allows you to help navigate discussions for a directed outcome.

For supervisors, it is about having an open ear to those you lead and encouraging feedback for the good of the organization. Also, it is about having respect for those around you, and valuing others enough to give them honest feedback. A culture of candor fights against organizational silence and helps teams develop and increase mission effectiveness.

Candor is not gossip. It is not lying. It is not slander. Speaking with candor has a purpose. It means to speak earnestly, honestly, and faithfully, and we can do this only as an outpouring of our internal character. An aid here is to ask these questions before speaking: is this necessary, is this loving, and is this truthful? Another helpful aid is to remember this acrostic:

Courageous words: *Having the courage to speak up and not giving in to fears about what others might think of you.*

Authenticity: *Telling others what you truly think, not simply what you think they want to hear.*

Navigating discussions: *Being an active participant in the flow of a conversation with candor helps to steer the conversation in a positive direction to obtain certain goals.*

Disclosing self: *Using courageous words and being authentic by allowing others to know what makes you tick.*

Openness to other ideas: *Exchanging ideas in an unintimidating way, especially for the leader who seeks to hear from all sides.*

Respect: *For leaders: soliciting and receiving candor well. For others: providing candor as a way of respecting leadership.*

Some might read the definition of candor above and decide they cannot be a person of candor if it requires those six items because they do not feel very brave or good at navigating discussions, while other people imbue these qualities naturally. Having candor does not require you to change who you are; it simply requires you to understand more about who you actually are, your true self, and letting others see this as well. It is about taking off the masks we all tend to wear and trust that honesty is always the right answer, instead of silent antipathy.

At one point in her career, Sammi could see that her boss was overworked and not trusting the staff to help accomplish the mission for the company. She built up the courage to meet with her supervisor and explain what she was witnessing. Although Sammi was authentic and showed respect, unfortunately, her candor was not received well, and the interaction damaged her relationship with her boss. She explained that this was a difficult life experience, and since then has second-guessed herself hundreds of times, wondering if she was respectful enough and truly had both her boss's and the company's best interests in mind. Months after her encounter, the board mandated that her boss take an emergency sabbatical so that the company could get back on track. Sammi was still there to assist in the process and felt somewhat vindicated. Though it did not go well at first, she was glad she had stepped up with courage when it was needed to help save the company.

In essence, candor flows from our character. The type of person we are—our inward life—is what enables us to speak with true candor because candor is a virtue of the heart. Patience, kindness, and a strong sense of right and wrong are all character traits

> **Our candor is either tethered to our character or to our ego.**

that, when rightly used (as with Sammi in the story above), could help save organizations from months of frustration. Unfortunately, however, our society has short-circuited this in conversational dynamics. People are quick to say things or post items on social media before the information is censored by their moral compass. This can cause a lot of relationship damage.

The reason candor is so misunderstood is because societal candor has become diseased. On any given day, the rhetoric flowing from our political leaders and entertainment icons provides what many might describe as candor, but is actually intolerant dogma— and no one likes a bully. True candor is never used as a disguise for personal gain. Crassness and name-calling has nothing to do with expressing candor. Candor without character is like a cancer; it can poison a conversation.

Our candor is either tethered to our character or to our ego, and we should pursue the former. In contrast, societal candor is often anchored in pride.

The following diagram illustrates the components of societal candor.

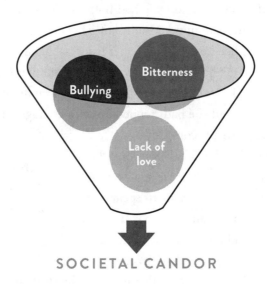

SOCIETAL CANDOR

Some might say, *Well, the truth hurts.* However, it is usually not the truth that hurts but the way the truth is packaged that hurts. Truth delivered in a sarcastic or mean-spirited way possesses barbs that inflict pain; sometimes the sole intention is to hurt the recipient. Lashing out with societal candor because of pride or anger is a type of "front-stabbing" that destabilizes relationships. Conversely, when the truth is presented from a person of character, at an appropriate time and with love, it will be more readily received.

The following illustration shows the proper elements of true candor.

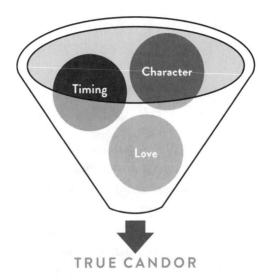

TRUE CANDOR

True candor is possible for all of us to achieve. But it will take some work. To shed light on this challenge, I have found the Bible to be a source of wisdom and relevant answers.

THE FOUR KEYS OF CANDOR

Many stories of candor in the Old Testament are associated with prophets.[5] In the New Testament, helpful verses related to the topic of candor are shared in the book of Ephesians. The apostle Paul encourages us to speak the truth in love and speak only the kind of words that are good for building up others, depending on their needs at that moment, so the words will benefit and give grace to the people who hear.[6]

These verses illustrate how to utilize candor. Candor, at its essence, is to speak truth, as a source of encouragement and according to the need of the moment, in order to give grace to the hearers.

Thus, an ancient letter written nearly two thousand years ago to a small congregation outlines for us a wonderful definition. Here, in summary, are the four keys to candor that will be used as a foundation for the rest of the book:

The Four Keys
1. Speak the unspoken truth
2. With love
3. When needed
4. To benefit others

As with the candor myths, it is important to understand what these four keys are *not* saying. We do not speak up in order to benefit ourselves. We should never speak up if it is to blow our own horn and to remind others of our accomplishments. That kind of candor is prideful. Also, the "with love" key cannot be sacrificed on the altar of justice. As we seek to "win our case," we must always think of the value and human dignity of those we confront. Sometimes it is easy to impose our own agenda on another person out of our desire to see them do well. This isn't actually loving.

• • •

We must always think of the value and human dignity of those we confront.

• • •

The third key is likewise critical. We are not to continually speak up, but only when necessary. We are not to be the conversation police. We are not to correct every wrong thing spoken. In attempting to do so, our need to ensure every fact, stat, and detail is thoroughly communicated takes precedence over loving the people with whom we are speaking. There is a fine line here. This means that having candor is not simply speaking up but understanding when it's appropriate and most helpful to do so.

Finally, what does it mean to give grace to those who hear? Essentially, this means to speak up in order to benefit others. Instead of showing malice toward others, we are to freely communicate love to them. This isn't easy and, depending on the setting, it might seem countercultural, but to love others and give grace is at the core of candor. We are to exhibit love and humility by tolerating obstinate people, though we are not to sit back and allow them to say things that are untrue or hurting the discussion. When there is a buffoon present, like a bee in the room you *have* to deal with it.

Anyone can state an opinion, but to speak the truth in love (key #2) is the quality that differentiates true candor. There is a deep-rooted connection between candor and love that is essential to understanding the importance of candor. Candor is always connected to something internally. Without love, candor becomes rooted in pride, fear, cynicism, or coldness—all enemies of candor (see the next chapter). With love, candor takes its rightful place in conversations.

Instead of an iron fist in a velvet glove, think of an open handshake. There is no hidden agenda or lethal force at work. In fact, it is the opposite. The lifesaving virtue of love is the operative force.

The following diagram represents the importance of fully possessing the qualities of both candor and love.

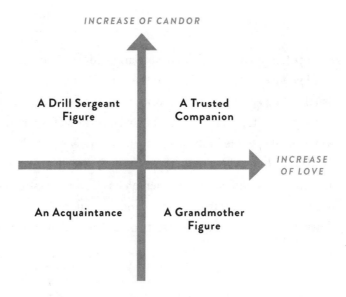

With an increase of love on the horizontal axis and an increase of candor on the vertical axis, we can derive four patterns of how people interact with each other. These four patterns of interaction are like four personality types, yet they are snapshots of relationships and do not necessarily mean that people will always perform within the same quadrant.

Here are the four patterns:

A. **Bottom left quadrant**. When a relationship displays low candor and low love, you typically have what I describe as an *Acquaintance* figure. These are the everyday people we meet: the server at Starbucks, the mechanic who rotates your tires, the people you may know in your community who are friendly but not friends. Though we should display kindness and compassion to all whom we meet, in the context of normal business-type transactions and social settings, there are limited opportunities for candor. Take time now to jot down the names of one or two people who are in this position in your life:

_____   _____

B. **Top left quadrant**. When a relationship displays high candor and low love, you typically have the *Drill Sergeant* figure. These are usually the people whose authority you may be under but may not be very close to, such as a sports coach or one of the executives at work. While people in these roles will naturally be candid with you, this leadership style is more transactional, directive, and autocratic. The higher level of authority a person has in your life, the more candor they will exhibit toward you—and with more immediacy. Write down the names of one or two people who are in this position in your life:

_____   _____

C. **Bottom right quadrant**. With low candor and high love, you are likely interacting with the *Grandmother* figure. These are the people in your life who love you unconditionally and may sugarcoat everything. This type could be representative of close friends or relatives who have a hard time telling you what they truly think, but they find it easy to express their love. Inherent in this type of relationship are those with codependent tendencies. Write down the names of one or two people who are in this position in your life:

_____   _____

D. **Top right quadrant**. Finally, when a relationship displays high candor and high love, this is the *Trusted Companion*. These are the people you can count on to be completely honest with you, yet provide feedback in a loving, nonjudgmental way. Like the little child in "The Emperor's New Clothes," they have nothing to lose with being completely honest, yet they share an unquestionable degree of love and trust with you. Write down the names of one or two people who are in this position in your life:

_____   _____

The relationship candor has with love is vital, yet some cultures have a particularly hard time adapting candor into the context of their relationships. Some people feel deeply discriminated against, exploited, and/or alienated. Some have a peculiar level of bitterness, helplessness, or hopelessness they have to work through on a daily basis. It's possible a lack of candor and love has exacerbated these issues.

What does it mean to speak the unspoken truth? It means I will share what is going on in me, not just what I want you to hear. When you are candid with someone you drop the barriers of your life. When you speak with candor it means you are creating intimacy. People are typically scared of intimacy. That is why we lie. Candor reverses this tendency. Speaking the unspoken truth also inherently means that there is definitely a tangible truth out there that most people can agree on. What you bring to the table is your perspective on that truth, and it is for the benefit of everyone in the room as long as it uses the four keys: speak up, with love, when needed, to benefit others. We particularly have to be careful of our motives and what drives us to speak. That is the focus of the next chapter.

* * *

At the conclusion of most chapters in this book, I offer a summary, candor strategies, questions, and an opportunity to make a commitment.

SUMMARY

Think of the story "The Emperor's New Clothes" as an illustration of human dynamics. Some leaders have not created a culture in which they will receive candid feedback. Employees often feel that if they speak the truth at work, they will be punished for it. Many times, however, the opposite occurs. When people speak with true candor (with love, when needed, in order to help), it is often received well, and the employee garners respect rather than being condemned.

Candor Strategies

1. Speak to people in private, if possible, especially if the subject matter is sensitive in nature and can be brokered without a group discussion.
2. Make it a point to engage the difficult topics. This is counterintuitive and seems dangerous. However, sometimes you have to go out on a limb because that is where the fruit is.
3. Go for gold. Speak about the most important issue that needs to be addressed. Sometimes the smaller items evaporate when the bigger ones are dealt with.

Reflection Questions

Write down the four keys of candor below:

1.

2.

3.

4.

Answer the following questions with the four keys in mind:

1. What is one area of your life where you need more candor?

2. How can you speak the unspoken truth in a loving way?

3. When would be the best time to speak up?

4. How would an open discussion benefit the relationship?

5. What is the difference between societal candor and true candor?

Please mark the following items true or false. Your answers to these statements can help you see more clearly how present candor is in your life now.

T / F In relationships I am open and honest and ask for feedback whenever possible.

T / F I provide an adequate amount of self-disclosure in my relationships.

T / F I do not hesitate to provide input when I hear something that does not sound quite right.

T / F I sometimes use camouflage to disguise what I am truly thinking and feeling.

CANDOR COMMITMENT

I commit to speaking the unspoken truth, with love, when needed, to benefit others!

CHAPTER 2

ENEMIES of CANDOR

There is no fear in love...[1]

Five years ago Chris Long of Reno, Nevada, received a bone marrow transplant. He was suffering from acute myeloid leukemia and myelodysplastic syndrome. Both of these conditions impaired his body's ability to create new blood, so he did not have a good prognosis. All that Long knew about the donor was that he was a younger man from Germany.

The transplant was an absolute success and saved Long's life. Yet something strange began to happen. Within just a few months, the DNA of Long's blood had changed to that of his donor. Long had become what is called a chimera—a person (or any living organism) that has two complete genomes, two sets of DNA. Long didn't realize it at the time, but his donor's DNA was slowly taking over his body. Now, four years later, most of his organs, and even his sperm, have the DNA of a younger man five thousand miles away.

Forensic scientists have taken a keen interest in Long's case. They realize that, if he committed a crime, any DNA he leaves at the crime scene or on a victim might point to an innocent man. As unreal as this story is—with a foreign DNA coming into a person's body, seeking dominance over the host DNA—we must remember that the host's condition was killing him. The DNA of a younger, healthier man was saving him.[2]

In one way, *societal* candor, with its bullying and bitterness, is diseased. It impairs our ability to create new and healthy relationships. In order to change this, we need radical chimera-like transformation. We need to intercept the "bad blood" and infuse unhealthy patterns of thought and action with new DNA that can change us, transform the way we speak to others, and benefit the communities to which we belong.

Personally, I have not been a consistent, sterling example of how to use candor. In the past, I have operated out of fear and have had to suffer the consequences. In fact, the story I shared in chapter 1 was permeated by a fear of losing my position. I debated for weeks about whether I should visit the board chairman at his home to tackle the issues I had with him one-on-one. However, I was afraid that before I had returned to my home and taken off my coat, he would have called the other board members to influence them to fire me. I didn't trust how he would have represented our private conversation to them.

Fear is candor enemy #1.

One of the things I feared the most in a private setting, even if I was caring toward him, is that the nature of the issues would cause my words to come across as severe. In the chairman's mind, I may have seemed an impertinent young man telling him off. A lack of trust, not only in him but also in the other board members, led me to challenge his nomination in a more open setting where there could be witnesses. Though the final results turned out okay, I believe that with additional courage, I could have circumvented some of the more public drama by speaking up as issues surfaced.

Fear is candor enemy #1 and must be eradicated. Fear, along with cynicism, a lack of confidence, and coldness, stand in direct opposition to the virtues of truth, trust, hope, and love. As with Long's transplant, our negative tendencies need to be rooted out and dealt with in order for us to express healthy candor and enjoy healthy relationships.

FEAR OF CANDOR

Who among us hasn't sat in a meeting, afraid of saying the wrong thing? *What if I get this wrong? What if this isn't what the conversation is really about? What if I say something and someone else makes fun of me?* Fear can lie dormant within us until we are faced with an opportunity to speak up and contribute something potentially important to an organization we care about. Then we choke and hedge our comments. Fear doesn't fight fair! Sometimes it makes us camouflage our true feelings or even lie because we do not want others to know the truth. Where does all this fear come from?

There is a self-preservation mechanism inside each of us, and one way it manifests itself is via the desire to be liked and admired. Some people display this more intensely than others. We might want to be recognized as being competent and gifted. We are scared that if other people find out who the *real me* is, they won't like or respect us. We know the truth . . . who we really are. We know our own personal weaknesses and failures. Even an acknowledgment that we desperately want to fit in and please others can be an embarrassment to us. *Shouldn't we be strong on the inside and not care what others think?*

The answer to that question is a qualified "no." We should care what others think about us, just not in a way that cripples our ability to be honest with them. It is important to be loved by other people; this is one of the most fulfilling areas of life. Yet, one of the components of love is honesty. It is not loving to disguise who we truly are. An action step that can be taken in response to fear and the other enemies of candor is to speak up, not in an effort to be noticed but to overcome the fear of being exposed.

How does one do that? First, be prepared to be open with others on a level that is uncharacteristic. Often, we're overly afraid of negative outcomes. But instead of focusing on risks, focus on results.

My daughters are very open with people about their faults and desire to be liked. As a result, others feel as if they know who my daughters really are; consequently, these young women have many intimate friendships. I have learned from them about being open and honest with others. For instance, if one of them says something and is criticized as being prideful, her response would be that she probably *is* too prideful and needs to work on that. Then she really does try to deal with it. It is refreshing to spend time with people so open and free with who they truly are.

Just as with individuals, organizations also suffer from fear. One of the issues that haunts companies is the focus on risks and failure. One candor strategy tool is to focus on results instead. Meetings can get bogged down in negative discussions, but we can utilize candor to remind others of potential rewards. For instance, in addition to looking at the risks, a leader with candor can cast a vision of greater gain that might increase morale and draw others into a more positive discussion.

CANDOR BECAUSE OF FEAR

Fear affects our ability to exercise proper candor in another way. People may communicate more candidly out of fear. What does that mean? Fear can promote an unhealthy candor. For instance, Kenny is one of thousands of employees climbing the ladder at a large corporation. He speaks with what many describe as great candor. The problem is that it is not loving, and it is not for the benefit of others at the appropriate moment. He tells people plainly what he thinks of them, and regularly tells coworkers what others have said about their performance. These practices have not endeared him to fellow employees.

The kind of candor Kenny displays offends people, and unfortunately, has not helped him in his career. He has been transferred from assignment to assignment, placing him in fierce competition with coworkers. He leaves a trail of hurt relationships among those he supervises. In their words, he has mastered the art of putting others down to build himself up.

Kenny was crushed when he found out that the higher-ups in his organization secretly did not like him and wanted to get rid of him. Instead of considering how he might have contributed to his leaders' negative impressions, he immediately lashed out and blamed other people. He couldn't accept the fact that he was not meeting his supervisors' expectations as a leader of their organization.

So what is going on with Kenny? He has some admirable traits, and he expresses his love to his family. If you were to ask him about his personality, he would own the fact that he is abrasive. The issue with Kenny is the same issue a lot of people struggle with: operating out of fear because of deep insecurities.

Kenny is afraid of the future, afraid of competition, and afraid he will be left behind. His type of candor is fueled by fear. Fear can take many forms, but at its root, in Kenny's case, it is the fear of being rejected, exposed, and abandoned. Because he does not have a positive sense of self-worth, he is unable to exercise candor out of a genuine love for others. Instead, devoid of self-awareness, he displays societal candor with its criticisms, bitterness, and bullying.

As a longtime chaplain in the US Army, I have counseled soldiers who were afraid of their spouses leaving them. Out of that fear, some became people they didn't want to be and used "candor" to pester their spouses about all their activities. Their fear of loss was a self-fulfilling prophecy, as their subsequent actions contributed to the division and ultimately led to separation. Their type of candor was their undoing. Like Kenny, the fear of rejection manifested itself in ways that, ironically, caused people to reject them. If this is something you see yourself struggling with, i.e. a crippling fear of rejection that results in banal, untimed honesty, then please keep reading. There is a better way, but first, there are additional enemies to address.

CYNICISM

One of the reasons people don't exercise candor is because of cynicism: cynicism with the current leadership, cynicism about the organization as a whole, or cynicism with the plan being discussed. At the core of cynicism is a lack of trust. Though they may not admit this or see it in themselves, a cynic is a person who does not believe in people or their plans. Ultimately, cynicism strips away candor because it tempts us to ask, "What is the point?"

A cynical person is skeptical about any number of things. Perhaps she believes other people are motivated solely by self-interest. Perhaps he is disenchanted with the system or thinks that he should be in charge. Whatever the case, a degree of pessimism or negativity has crippled an individual's ability to collaborate or to lead with candor.

This is displayed in meetings when someone is physically present but is mentally "checked out." Cynics display much more than apathy, however. Cynicism is active negativity and contributes nothing to meetings. It is a negative emotion. It sucks the enthusiasm out of others who are present, impeding them from seeing what could actually be.

One of the places you would expect to have hopeful and positive people is in a faith community. Is it even possible to be a cynical person of faith? Seems oxymoronic. However, there is cynicism even in organized religion. People feel let down by their church or synagogue, the leaders of their denomination, or even by God Himself. A lack of trust grows into a pessimistic attitude that can rob joy not only from the cynic, but from those around them.

There is far more cynicism in a regular work environment. For instance, a person may hang around for years to receive a promotion they desperately want and think they deserve. Yet, when the job goes to someone else, cynicism sets in and soon they are communicating their disappointment by making negative comments during business meetings. Other people believe that everyone is trying to take advantage of them or get away with something, which can lead to hostile cynicism.

LACK OF CONFIDENCE

A lack of confidence can also erode one's ability to speak up when necessary. The confidence needed is not based on our accomplishments, intellect, or status; it is gained in truly knowing who we are and being comfortable with ourselves. This is easier said than done. Some people have been through tragedies and others were never provided with a good example to follow. Everyone approaches life differently based on their past experiences, and fear of failure is a huge part of lacking confidence. *What if I fail? What if I don't measure up? What if they see the real me? What if I say the wrong thing?*

These issues are real and will be addressed head-on in chapter 5. For now, it is important to ask yourself if you have a confidence deficit. Could it be because of a crippling fear of rejection? Sometimes we can assume an entire group is thinking something hateful about us. In our anxiety, we can make problems worse for ourselves than they need to be.

We all know people who appear to live life with ease, energy, and positivity; their careers, their transitions in life, and their relationships seem to always begin on a firm footing and move forward with a sure spirit. It looks appealing, yet impossible for us . . . *that can only be a life for them, right?* No, this is not true. It is possible to gain the confidence you need to go about your daily business without fear.

For some people, their faith practices aid in an understanding of who they are in the big picture of life, and this assists them in keeping perspective. For others it might be the traditions they learned from family members. Whatever the case, learning to have confidence—and it *is* something you can learn—tackles head-on one of the enemies of candor.[3]

A lack of confidence inhibits candor because forthright honesty must spring from somewhere. Confidence is assuredly a deep well from which candor pours forth. My confidence, as a chaplain, is in the Lord. Knowing that I am not in this alone is amazingly helpful when I am in tough situations and have to speak with candor.

COLDNESS (OR A LACK OF LOVE)

Another great enemy of candor is simply a lack of love or a coldness of heart toward others. Much is written about love in modern society, but what happens when you don't feel it? What happens when you discover a chilliness in your heart toward the plight of others?

Many years ago, as a theological student in the Chicago area, I suffered from a lack of love. I was going to school full time to learn the deep truths of the Bible, including, of course, all about God's love for His people. But I struggled to love my neighbors. I had four children, worked a graveyard shift as a security guard, and every day I felt I had exceeded my maximum emotional capacity.

I knew I was supposed to know my neighbors and care for them, but it was difficult. I had very little extra time to be neighborly and hang around outside in order to strike up a relationship. I certainly didn't feel love for my neighbors, and I didn't feel like I had time or energy to give it. Thankfully, I recognized there was a coldness in my attitude and sought to do something about it.

I prayed about my lack of love, and there were some unique breakthroughs, to the point that it was tough to say goodbye after three years there. For instance, my wife and I started a weekly home group study with neighbors who contributed toward a meal, and we grew close with those who participated.

There are times in life when we feel we have nothing to give or, more concerning, we completely lack the desire to give or to do the right thing.

Some people don't struggle over their lack of love for others. Their attitudes are more along the lines of, *You live your life, let me live mine.* Such feelings are an enemy to candor. It is hard to speak the truth in love when you don't love the people with whom you're speaking.

This is what makes the instructions from the apostle Paul so critical. It is not just, "If you have nothing good to say, don't say anything." That kind of attitude and thinking breeds cynicism. The better precept is, "Say what you need to say—good or bad—but say it in a way that communicates love to the receiver." Part of love is communication. It is more loving to speak up than to sit and stew on an issue in the presence of others.

All through life we are told to love others. It does not seem optional. Is it abnormal not to instinctually have a great love for others? Not necessarily, and there are steps we can take to increase in love. When we don't have love, we can pray for it. We can go ahead and act lovingly, doing what we know we are supposed to do, and trust that our affections will grow as a result of these loving actions. Many see love merely as an emotion they must feel in order to act, but it is possible to act lovingly even when the feelings are not present.

Although it seems like the forces that constrain candor are numerous, you can overcome candor's enemies with the help of the two things we'll discuss next: love and trust.

LOVE—FEAR'S GREAT ANTIDOTE

I have regretted moments in my life when I played it safe because of fear: afraid to speak up, afraid to do the right thing, afraid of the future. But I have learned that, when we are driven by love, our fears fall to the wayside. When I lead with love, there is no fear keeping me back. It's almost as if when we are blinded with love, we cannot see what once might have corrupted us. The apostle John said that "perfect love casts out fear."[4]

Similarly, when we speak up to others or for others out of our love for them, we move from being that grandmother figure or acquaintance to becoming a trusted companion. When we speak candor into others' lives out of love, we can truly help them, and it helps us. It strengthens us, builds relationships, and makes all of us more courageous.

Think again about Kenny. To give him the benefit of the doubt, perhaps he was able to show love to his family and be vulnerable when he was with them. However, he was never vulnerable in the workplace; it was too risky there. Loving others requires vulnerability, and some people refuse to display this where they work. Kenny always had to be right. He had to be seen as right, and he would argue the point and hold a grudge with anyone who disagreed with him. He confounded others with his arrogant statements. None of these actions were loving.

Recall the graph from chapter 1 describing the importance of love and candor working in tandem with each other to produce a good result (relationships based on trust). Instead of operating from love, Kenny used his position to operate out of his authoritative power as illustrated in the diagram below:

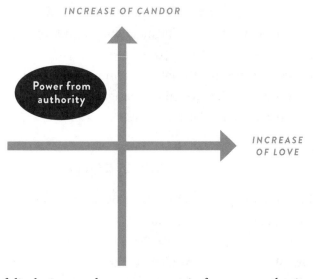

Instead of displaying candor as a power trip from our authority, as shown above, the goal is a mixture of love and candor that produces an authority from your relational investments. This kind of power is built by giving others the two things they really need: honesty and love. It is an authority seasoned with friendliness, possesses a confidence with closeness, and has an assurance balanced with an affection for others, as seen in the graph below.

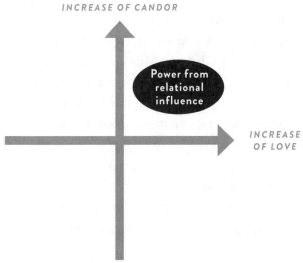

A love for others also conquers cynicism. When we love others, we trust them, hope for them, and hope with them. Again we can look to the apostle Paul: "[Love] bears all things, believes all things, hopes all things, [and] endures all things."[5] Cynicism vanishes when we unleash our love for others. Besides love, there is another avenue by which to escape the fear trap.

THE POWER OF TRUST

I heard it said once that we judge ourselves by our motives, but we judge others by their behavior.[6] It's true: we give ourselves way more slack than we give to others. For instance, if I mess up, I commonly say, "Well, it was not my intent to do this. It was not my intent to say [that comment] and hurt others." Yet, I rarely give anyone else the same benefit of the doubt. Instead, I immediately assume they were intending harm all along or scheming to make my life more miserable.

• • •

Trust is integral to the process of transferring from diseased societal candor to healthy, loving candor.

• • •

This is where trust comes in. It is not blind faith; rather, it's simply mastering the ability to give others the same grace that I give to myself. When we hear things from others that do not sound right, instead of stewing about it or gossiping about it with others, we clarify it. We trust that others have the same good intentions we do.

Trust is integral to the process of transferring from diseased societal candor to healthy, loving candor. With trust we can learn to come into situations of relating to others without any prejudging or stereotypes, past grudges, or feelings of fear or cynicism. With trust, as with love, we enter the arena fresh and ready to tackle whatever lions may come our way.

Candor can open the door of trust in ways we may not expect. The following is a story about a student and his professor that shows how trust can change an outcome. My brother Nathanael now works as a senior executive in a large organization; but many years ago, something happened that helped him get to where he is today. In college, his fear once nearly kept him from telling the truth because of the cost involved. He realized he could put his fear aside and speak with candor. The experience shaped him.

I was a first year student at Georgia Tech (1st quarter actually). I was taking my first calculus class. The professor was not particularly good . . . did not explain things well. We had an exam scheduled. I felt unprepared, so I skipped class that day. I went to the next class session, apologized for missing the previous class, and asked him if I could take a makeup test. He looked at me and asked, "What happened? Were you sick?" Ugh! It never occurred to me that he would ask! It would have been so easy to lie, but something inside compelled me to be honest. I said something like, "I'll be honest with you. I wasn't sick, but I didn't feel prepared to take the test." I braced for him to tell me too bad, so sad. But to my surprise, he said, "Well, that normally would not be a good excuse, but I will let you take the makeup this time." I was greatly relieved and managed to pass the course with an honorable "C." I was afraid to tell the truth, but I learned a great lesson that day that stuck with me throughout college and my career.

Thankfully my brother decided to be forthright and honest with his professor, who, appreciating his candor, cut him some slack and extended grace. This small event helped shape Nathanael into the man he is today. This story not only speaks to the need for candor, but about how giving people the benefit of the doubt can make a lasting impression.

In summary, if we could count the cost of what we have lost in life due to fear, we would be done with fear immediately. Our lives were meant to count for something. Love and trust are two reins whereby we can override fear and make the most out of life.

Enter the arena with candor.

Lead with love.

Live with trust.

Make life count.

The following chapters will confront the enemies of candor straight on and provide many tangible ways to bring love, truth, and trust into all of your relationships.

SUMMARY

There are many reasons why people do not speak up more often. This chapter exposed a few of the major areas that keep people from communicating more: cynicism, lack of confidence, and coldness (lack of love). One of the greatest enemies of candor is fear. Fear is what fuels a lack of trust. Sometimes we are afraid of getting hurt. Sometimes we are anxious about what others might think of us. Sometimes we wonder if our ideas are truly valuable or not. Love and trust fight these enemies of candor, and true candor increases as our ability to lead in love increases.

Strategies for Overcoming Fear

1. Instead of focusing on risks, focus on results. Resist the temptation to be overly afraid of negative outcomes.
2. Avoid the word "just." It shows weakness or, worse, a passive-aggressive nature. For instance, "If you could just redo that presentation for me to make it better . . ." Simply ask or tell someone to do something. Using the word *just* belies the task, making it sound simple, even when you are asking something

that might be challenging. Using the word *just* does not display candor.

3. Love others generously. Show the other person through your tone and facial expression that you care about him or her.

Reflection Questions

Write some of the enemies of candor below:

1.

2.

3.

4.

Answer the following questions:

1. Are there any other issues which might contribute to a lack of candor? If so, what are they?

2. Describe a situation where you displayed a fear of speaking up.

3. What are the ways you have displayed cynicism in the last month?

4. Describe a situation where you suffered from a lack of confidence during a conversation.

CANDOR COMMITMENT

I commit to identifying the enemies of candor in myself and defeating them with love and trust!

CHAPTER 3

LEADERS and MEETINGS with CANDOR

All faults may be forgiven of him who has perfect candor.[1]

—WALT WHITMAN

Landon works for a government agency and slogs to work each day via a challenging commute. He is the assistant of a senior supervisor who routinely displays negative leadership qualities and knowingly causes anxiety in her employees. The company performed an assessment of their staff to determine the climate and morale of the workforce. Many of the respondents indicated the supervisor was to blame for the poor morale. When Landon met with his supervisor about the results, she told him she was confused by the feedback. She wanted Landon to form a committee to determine how the scores could be raised.

Landon sat in bewilderment. His supervisor was not taking any ownership of the low assessment results—some of which directly pointed out her weaknesses. Instead, she wondered what everyone else could do to fix the problem. Landon struggled to express candor with her. He feigned some confusion himself so he could ask her the obvious question: How could "we" employees fix a problem centered on "her" leadership? He used this tactic to see what she might say, but she did not take the bait. His lack of courage and candor kicked his problems down the road instead of helping him, his coworkers, or his supervisor.

The common workplace needs candor to survive. So do our government, our schools, our military, our churches, and our city councils. Organizations without candor are dragged down by a lack of honesty and open communication. They limp along doing some of the same things over and over because no one is brave enough to raise their hand and ask the "why" question. It is an ongoing problem at many companies.

Other organizations *with* candor, such as Motorola and General Electric as mentioned before, grow and evolve in ways no one thought possible. Leaders who seek out and value the opinions of employees receive more feedback, and in the process uplift those around them. Individuals bloom, and those who exhibit appropriate candor are also seen as leaders and often promoted.

In the worst case, a lack of candor can lead to hypocrisy, bitterness, lying, gossip, and downright division. But lives with candor keep things interesting, expectant, truthful, and exploratory. Candor helps to build relationships by using courage, vulnerability, and feedback. It leverages openness and honesty to increase trust, bringing greater value to organizations and relationships. But this environment cannot be created when there is fear.

The moment a leader allows fear to enter the workplace, he or she has set the stage for the shared mission to plateau, or worse, decline. When people are afraid to speak up to their supervisors about how things might work better, a stifled culture develops. Coworkers then speak to each other about what needs to be corrected and they complain about the boss and the unhealthy work climate. Supervisors need to remain accessible, open to suggestions, and not critical— even with feedback they disagree with.

This chapter is divided into several parts: the first few sections will be more useful for the leader; and the final sections will be useful to those required to participate in organizational meetings. This chapter will also illustrate principles on how to thrive in the meeting environment.

LEADERSHIP AND CANDOR

One crucial aspect of being a leader is that you have to feel comfortable in your own shoes, meaning who you have become as a person. You cannot get immediately offended when people speak the unspoken truth, no matter how much you think the information reflects poorly on you. I have spoken to people in large organizations and small community groups where they believed it was the leader who had the most impact on creating an environment of trust and on leveraging candor to unlock new pathways to succeed.

Take, for instance, Anna, now retired, who worked for a technology company for her entire career. The programs her team rolled out impacted tens of thousands of people. For years, Anna felt incredibly valued by her leadership team, and when they held creative meetings, her high level of candor was appreciated and taken in the right spirit. However, as she advanced, there was a new leadership team to please along with a mix of people she had not worked with before. Her opinions and candid feedback were not as appreciated. In fact, she began to receive negative performance reviews.

Anna felt like a victim of her own success. She had been promoted into a high-level team of people who, in her opinion, were struggling to get things done, partly because they were too sensitive and thin-skinned. She was forced to attend a series of six counseling sessions because of her poor peer reviews. Anna began to question herself and not only her role in the company but her entire personality as well.

What was truly going on? Anna was experiencing a breakdown of trust among teammates to the point where even backstabbing was happening high on the corporate ladder. Her new leaders were not as comfortable in their position in the company and began to wonder if members of their team who spoke up a lot, like Anna, were secretly gunning for their positions.

Is this a common issue? In our earlier example, Gretchen experienced a similar situation. When she attempted to speak up and provide her point of view, she was reprimanded and told that she had lost credibility. She was also threatened and told she could lose the directorship of the program she was leading.

What is going on here? What type of leader is so insecure that he or she cannot tolerate the truth? Unfortunately, this is more often the norm than the exception. In my military career, I have made comments in an effort to provide forthright honesty in a respectful way, only to be told that if I said anything like that again, I would be disciplined. One of my leaders tapped my chest and said I was just a major. He hinted that if I did not change my ways, he would ruin my career.

At best, this type of leader is one whom I would call a *transactional* leader, one who is high in candor but low in trust and understanding. At worst, this type of leader is one many would call toxic. They operate by ruling others and are more directive and autocratic.

The opposite is a *trainwreck* leader who is more reactive. They care about you, but they are driven by feelings and can change direction like the wind. They do not intentionally set out to wreck people's lives; however, their subordinates often feel as if the sand is constantly shifting under their feet. Employees routinely do not know if they are on the right path or not because their emotional leader changes course—sometimes to please their own bosses or even their employees. They may let things take their own course, and they are not intentional, which can be dangerous in a rapidly changing environment.

A third type of leader—the *transformational* leader—is one who has the right mixture of candor and love. These are the leader of leaders who care about you and the organization deeply, but their care does not interfere with their decision-making. They are more reflective and inspirational. They can appear to be democratic in their decision-making because they do so well at bringing others into the planning; yet, they alone make the final decision.

Here is a derivative of the quad diagram from chapter 1 to summarize these three types of leaders.

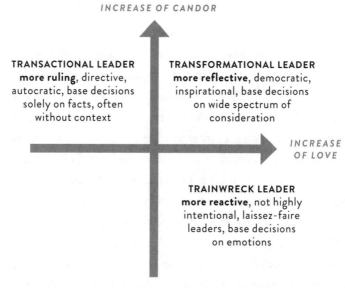

INCREASE OF CANDOR

TRANSACTIONAL LEADER
more ruling, directive, autocratic, base decisions solely on facts, often without context

TRANSFORMATIONAL LEADER
more reflective, democratic, inspirational, base decisions on wide spectrum of consideration

INCREASE OF LOVE

TRAINWRECK LEADER
more reactive, not highly intentional, laissez-faire leaders, base decisions on emotions

Now it is time to get a little deeper. What kind of leader are you? I know it is a personal question. Are you a leader who is offended when honest comments are made during your meetings? Are you a leader who listens to those whom you lead? Are you the type of leader who gives and receives feedback appropriately?

THE LEADERSHIP FEEDBACK LOOP

Businessman Jack Welch was the chairman and CEO of General Electric Company from 1981 to 2001. During that time, GE's value rose over 4,000 percent.[2] One reason he attributes to his success is that he promoted candor in the workplace. He said:

> I would call lack of candor the biggest dirty little secret in business.
> What a huge problem it is. Lack of candor basically blocks smart ideas, fast action, and good people contributing all the stuff they've got. It's a killer.
> When you've got candor—and you'll never completely get it, mind you—everything just operates faster and better.[3]

Welch found in candor a pathway to success for his company, and the results cannot be ignored. In essence, it does not matter what kind of organization you are leading; whether it be business, governmental, military, ministry, political, or community-based, candor has value in your workplace and is of great worth to you. As the leader, you might understand more than anyone else what is important for the organization to succeed—especially if you have been there awhile—but you cannot see everything. As your organization grows and becomes more complex, it is increasingly important to understand the dynamics that are taking place at the lowest level and all through the ranks. Leaders who do not value this information do not last long and the mission can soon steer off course.

The diagram below illustrates the conversation flow in a healthy work environment.

LEADERSHIP FEEDBACK LOOP

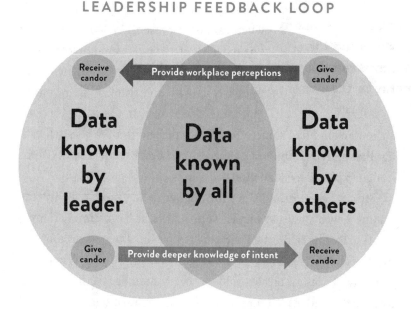

The illustration displays how information is shared amongst parties. There is actually another bubble that could be included: *data not known to anyone*; but it would take us outside the scope of this discussion.

The arrow at the top of the diagram shows that in a healthy work environment, data known by others—the team—flows to the leader through candor when he or she positions themselves to receive workplace perceptions. This is crucial. This is how a leader understands what is happening at the grass roots.

The arrow on the bottom is also an important piece of conversation flow. The leader provides candor to the team so that they gain a deeper understanding of why decisions are made. The leader models how to receive candor when he accepts input graciously. Team members, in turn, are provided a blueprint for how to process that information, even if at first it appears critical.

Candor is generally avoided by leaders and organizations because it sometimes creates discomfort. Well-established lines of authority

● ● ●

The strongest leaders understand that sometimes good is the enemy of the best.

● ● ●

might appear to be temporarily in jeopardy when candor is present. Welcoming candor opens a leader to a certain amount of vulnerability because if there is anything perceived to be wrong with an organization, it reflects on that leader. However, the strongest leaders understand that sometimes good is the enemy of the best,[4] meaning that a certain amount of success can bring contentment, which can quickly lead to stagnation.

More of everything is not the answer; being more effective and finding new avenues to impact your market is. Sometimes an organization that has plateaued needs a creative burst to make it continue to grow and thrive. This is where candor comes into play. When used properly, it communicates value to every member of the team, including the leader. Candor is critical to successful organizations.

THE CHARACTER OF THE LEADER

Before we discuss specific skills a leader might possess in order to have highly effective teams, let's address the essential quality for every leader—character. In my years of serving in the army and in serving nonprofit ministry organizations, I have witnessed several good, and also several horrific, leadership styles. The fountain from which each one of the two styles flowed was character.

What is character? Character is most clearly exhibited in people who have a strong sense of right and wrong. They do not take the unethical shortcut and are conscientious to ensure that no one is being cheated, including the company. Character is morality or uprightness; a person of character lives by the ethics he or she embraces.

Another element of character is represented in a person's compassion for others and concern with the meaningful areas of life, such as faith, family, country, community service, and caring for others. Lastly, a person who has character is someone whose life is marked with virtues. Many of the virtues described in the book of Proverbs in the Bible would be true of the person of character, such as keeping promises.

Let's take this discussion a little deeper. Character helps people keep their commitments; but in another sense, a person's character *informs* the commitments that he or she makes. It serves as the moral compass to help a person make commitments to the right things and not to the wrong things. All the commitments we make are a reflection of our character.

Taking this idea one step further, it is our commitments that propel our candor. Because of the commitments we have made and the importance they have in our lives, we are impelled to improve them and make them the best they can be, and not just because we want a good investment of our time and resources. We want to belong to meaningful institutions that are impacting people and changing the world. This motivation gives us the impetus for candor, and the result is that our candor becomes an outward display of our character and our commitment.

The intricate relationships between our character, commitments, and candor are evident:

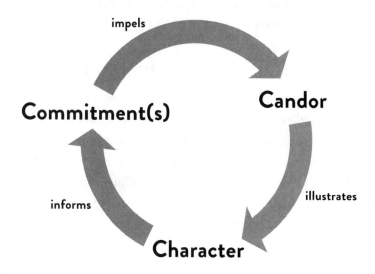

As you can see from the diagram, our character informs our commitments; our commitment to someone or something impels our candor; and our candor, in turn, is an illustration of our character. How we treat people matters. When we are honest with them and graciously accept their honesty at face value, it displays a level of character in our lives. For clarity, let's define these three terms: Character, Commitment, and Candor.

CHARACTER	COMMITMENT(S)	CANDOR
• Strong sense of right and wrong • Morality or uprightness • Actions resemble ascribed ethics • Compassion/ Concern • Life marked with virtues	• Follows through on promises • Resolve to do something • Mental affirmations • Obligations	• Forthright honesty • Openness • Frankness • Truthfulness • Sincerity

We are not done looking at character. The final chapter of this book is devoted to achieving character instead of charm and finding a balance on how to utilize candor in the context of trusting relationships, instead of elevating self.

CANDOR SKILLS FOR THE LEADER

In chapter 1, I outlined how to provide candor. Receiving candor involves a different set of rules. The listener should be patient in hearing out the other person; resist the temptation to interrupt or provide excuses; embrace any discomfort that comes with the candor (because it might bring an awkward feeling into the room); be appreciative; and never question the speaker's motive.

Here is a summary for the leader of both giving and receiving candor:

Giving Candor (from chapter 1)

1. Speak the unspoken truth
2. With love
3. When needed
4. To benefit others

Receiving Candor

1. Be patient
2. Listen attentively with an open mind
3. Embrace the discomfort
4. Be appreciative
5. Believe the best of the speaker and their motives

We'll now break down each of the five ways for a leader to receive candor.

Be patient: First, be patient because you cannot read another person's mind. Even if you think you know where they are going with an idea, you'll likely be surprised because of the uniqueness of every individual. We have a tendency to put people into a box and believe that everything that's important to know about them is known. This is never the case. Nothing stifles a person faster than having someone display the pretense that you already know what they are going to say. It is like the friend who rushes you at the end of your sentence (*yeah, yeah, yeah!*), signaling they got the point and they are ready to move on. This behavior squelches the entire conversation. A lack of patience can be somewhat amplified in digital communications such as texting.

The other day, a friend of mine told me something via text and I replied. He completely misread my response, or the tone of what I was saying, and nearly flew into a rage until I explained that he had inferred something in my text message I didn't intend. An additional text could clarify, but most people are too rushed, and instead jump to conclusions. Impatience, whether among friends or leaders and their team members, can damage relationships. This leads into step 2.

Listen attentively with an open mind: When put in a tough spot, it is easy to feel defensive, but resist the temptation to interrupt or provide excuses. As mentioned, we tend to give ourselves far more slack than we give to others. Listening with an open mind isn't easy. I sometimes feel I have to step outside of myself and tell myself to pay attention. This is the opportunity to allow others to state their case without interrupting them or becoming personally offended by what they say.

Embrace the discomfort: Many times, the advent of candor produces awkwardness until a culture of candor is created. With this awkwardness comes feelings of needing to change the topic or, for instance, to stop a meeting. Instead, embrace the awkwardness and don't allow the discomfort to torpedo a good discussion. Not everything can be pre-programmed and presented with professionalism. When candor is present, there can be a feeling that the ship is sinking, but that is not the case. Work through it. Embrace the awkwardness.

Be appreciative: The fourth step in receiving candor from others is to be appreciative and value what they are saying, as though it is a gift. When someone speaks up when I am leading a meeting, I have learned to appreciate the fact they feel free to do so. Often, the first reaction is *why are you doing this to me?* But when you see candor as an opportunity to bring health and a more effective strategy to the mission, then appreciation is the right response.

Believe the best of the speaker and their motives: Lastly, we have to believe the best of the speaker and resist the temptation to question the speaker's motives. Our minds can run wild, it is true, especially when we are being challenged, but it is imperative to give others the benefit of the doubt. We are sometimes left in the dark as to why certain people say the things they do, and that is okay. A leader's posture is to be *for* others, so they can give subordinates a little clearance when difficult topics come up. Not everyone is out to get us. Think of Anna and the blowback she received from an insecure leader. May this not be the trap we fall into.

Now that we have defined how to go about receiving candor, one last question still remains: how do leaders go about soliciting candor and developing an overall culture of candor? This is actually easy to answer. Ask lots and lots of questions. Provide opportunities to receive feedback and input, both during structured time and during non-structured time. Leaders never have to ask permission to engage others about issues, and are not afraid of hearing the raw truth. Good leaders take in as much data as possible. Having an open door policy should not be just a slogan but a real work practice for leaders to hear from their employees. Taking the initiative with this will set the stage for a culture of candor.

SKILLS FOR TEAM MEMBERS

Now that we have discussed the leader's role with candor, we turn to team members who must often endure long meetings. Everyone knows it can be a challenge to sit in meeting after meeting, patiently wondering how valuable the investment of time may be. One of the ways to avoid this discomfort is to provide candor to your leaders. If the meetings do not apply to you, but you are required to attend, have you ever told your leadership team that it would be a better use of your time not to attend? This type of feedback is one way to encourage even the most powerful leader to become more self-aware and pause to consider how seemingly simple decisions affect their team members.

The information in the beginning of this chapter suggested ways for leaders to learn more about receiving candor in the workplace. The following suggestions are for team members to enhance facilitating candor with their leaders:

1. Don't take responsibility for trying to change your boss; instead, consider how to sensitively communicate your needs and ideas.
2. Instead of confronting your boss, look for opportunities that open the door for a discussion on leadership, such as a climate survey.[5]
3. Try to spend time together in nonconfrontational areas, rather than in a board room or office. Meet for lunch. Go for a walk. Grab a coffee. The more time you can spend developing trust, the better.
4. Work on incorporating team activities to get to know each other and develop trust.
5. When meeting for a performance review, ask your supervisor to explore ways with you on how to increase candor.
6. Ask your boss if your team could spend one half-day a month on leadership development. Invite speakers or read a book together on leadership during the month, then discuss it. Many leaders want to be known as one who mentors and develops other leaders.

I once had a supervisor I was not getting along with. It seemed like he always had a snarky remark for me or was short with me. I longed for a better relationship, but he was a little intimidating to be around. One day I asked him if we could spend time getting to know each other better. Perhaps we could grab a Coke and sit outside at the picnic table for a half hour once in a while. He looked at me and said, "You're in charge of the office calendar, schedule it." So I did. We met several times and discussed a lot—things about work and things about our personal lives. After those meetings, there was a marked improvement in our work relationship.

Leaders need candor from their teams. It is lifesaving to the organization for them to hear from their subordinates. At the same time, subordinates need to position themselves to receive candor from their leaders. As the example below illustrates, giving and receiving candor works both ways.

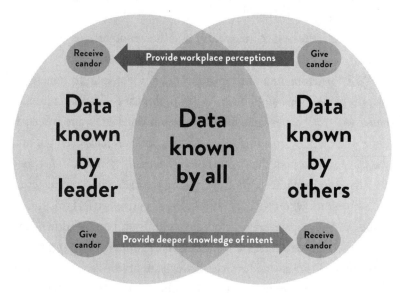

This time we'll focus on the arrow at the bottom of the illustration. Another exchange of candor happens when a supervisor provides guidance to his or her team. Just as it is important for a leader to provide candor, it is important for team members to receive candor from leaders. This can be about the organization as a whole, or about the subordinate's personal work, such as during a mid-year review. This interaction allows employees to learn more about the mission and hear some of the hidden reasons for the leader's words and actions. In any well-run organization, the leader's intent is an essential part of mission development.

The guidelines for team members in receiving candor vary slightly from those discussed earlier.

Receiving Candor

1. Be present (fully engaged, hearing what the speaker is saying)
2. Have faith in yourself
3. Listen attentively and receive what the speaker says
4. Be authentic and honest when given the opportunity to respond
5. Believe the best of the speaker and their motives

When listening to and receiving candor, it is helpful to remember that the person speaking—a supervisor in this case—is another human being who may experience many of the same struggles and insecurities at their job as you and your coworkers do. They have been put into their position to help the organization. Listening keenly to what they are saying and not interpreting everything as a critique is helpful here.

Sometimes when we hear something negative, we feel misunderstood, and perhaps even targeted; then our listening shuts down, and we can tend to dehumanize our leaders, e.g., *another over-promoted boss out for themselves.* However, if we listen objectively, noting they are people—with many of the same gifts and/or issues—trying to communicate something valuable, we can better absorb important data. Too often, we defensively focus on ourselves, our visible work outcomes, our future career, etc., instead of truly hearing and understanding what our supervisors may be communicating. Here are some final questions a team member might ask their supervisor to facilitate candor (#1 is mentioned in an earlier paragraph):

1. Is it necessary for me to be part of this meeting?
2. Please remind me of the reasons this meeting was scheduled.
3. What would be the most important outcomes from this meeting in your perspective?
4. What else would you like me to know?

In conclusion, employees should resist the urge to tell their leaders what they think they want to hear. Organizations pay big money for external assessments of how they are truly operating. Good leaders look to their subordinates to provide honest feedback. It is incumbent on all employees to follow the first rule of candor and to *speak the truth*. It is not okay to speak about the leadership issues at your workplace with coworkers, yet not engage leaders with candor in an effort to change things.

The military great George C. Marshall tells the story of what he experienced when he offered honest feedback to WWI leader General John J. Pershing:

I have never seen a man who could listen to so much criticism—as long as it was constructive criticism and wasn't just being irritable or something of that sort. You could talk to him like you were discussing somebody in a different country and yet you were talking about him personally . . . . You could say what you pleased as long as it was straight, constructive criticism. Yet he did not hold it against you for an instant. I never saw another commander that I could do that with. Their sensitivity clouded them up, so it just wouldn't work. I have seen some I could be very frank with, but I never could be frank to the degree that I could with General Pershing.[6]

SUMMARY

The everyday workplace needs candor to survive. Candor helps to build professional relationships by using courage, vulnerability, and feedback. It leverages openness and honesty to increase trust. It brings greater value to organizations, corporations, churches, and other community groups. Following the guidelines and steps to both give and receive candor can help facilitate communication, trust, and openness in any setting.

Strategies for the Workplace

1. Resist the temptation to tell people simply what you think they want to hear. Tell others what they need to hear. Avoid the urge to be a people pleaser.
2. Don't be overly concerned about the impression you are making; try to find the most truthful and helpful points to the discussion.
3. Follow-up your candor when the meeting concludes. Your words may not have been taken in the way you meant them, or you may have said the wrong thing. Follow-up and readdress the issue as soon as possible when needed.
4. Attack the problem, not the personality. Give others the benefit of the doubt. Communicate out of an abundance of trust until you are proven wrong.

Reflection Questions

1. Have you ever experienced feeling misunderstood in the workplace like Anna or Gretchen? What did you do about it?

2. Recall the three types of leaders: Transactional, Trainwreck, and Transformative. For leaders: Based on your understanding of this chapter, which type of leadership style have you displayed in the past? Do you sway more to the love category or the candor category? For team members: Which type of leader are you currently working with? What guidelines might you apply under this type of leadership?

3. For leaders: Do you regularly ask for feedback from your subordinates? How might you receive it in a more appropriate way? For team members: Do you regularly offer candor to your supervisor? How might you give it in a more appropriate way?

CANDOR COMMITMENT

I am committed to my organization; therefore, I will give and receive candor when needed. I also commit to giving others the benefit of the doubt and resisting the temptation to tell others simply what I think they want to hear.

CHAPTER 4

CANDOR in FAMILIES

If we are not ashamed to think it, we should not be ashamed to say it.[1]

—ATTRIBUTED TO MARCUS TULLIUS CICERO

One of the underlying problems in communication amongst family members is often the same problem in an organizational setting: a lack of trust. As a chaplain, I have counseled soldiers for nearly twenty years and, alongside my wife, have led hundreds of couples through marriage conferences and workshops; yet, I am still discovering the deep truths about the significance of trust. When it comes to marriage and family relationships, trust and commitment must be the foundation for there to be any hope for success.

This means people must be honest with each other and live lives of integrity. We cannot say one thing and then do another. The people we live with see everything. Those who know us best know when we are being hypocritical. They can tell simply from the expression on our face when things are not good, when we are fibbing, and when we are not listening.

Candor is the perfect accompaniment to healthy family relationships. Sometimes we miss the easiest things, those right in front of us. When Tony Miltenberger and I researched and wrote the marriage book *Unbreakable*, we were shocked at how a simple thing like kindness could be so incredibly beneficial to a marriage. We also discovered this about honesty. Indeed, some of the basic building blocks of life—items readily available to any couple—can easily repair and strengthen our significant relationships. Honesty, forthrightness, listening, and forgiveness are essential ingredients to build healthy relationships.

In this chapter, we will identify several ways that we can utilize candor to strengthen our marriages and support us in being better parents. Knowing the child-parent relationship can be a challenge at any age, I will also touch on how we can utilize candor with our own parents. I trust this study will be beneficial to you as you seek to succeed at fortifying these critical relationships of life.

CANDOR IN MARRIAGE

If I were to ask you what was the largest issue troubling your marriage, what would you say? Money, sex, in-laws, teenage children, limited time together? I know that these five responses identify about 90 percent of the issues for common couples. How can candor help? All of these issues have something in common—negotiation. Finances have to be brokered. Boundaries with in-laws need to be discussed. Issues regarding sex and time together can be worked out—in most cases—through honest discussion and a strengthening of trust.

Of course, some people have spouses with serious, possibly diagnosable, issues that require counseling and a lot of prayer and support. Take, for instance, Jan. Without her knowledge, Jan's husband applied for credit cards and made purchases to the extent that his actions have ruined their credit and placed the family on the brink of bankruptcy. Though money might be considered the main issue, a lack of honesty and forthrightness has caused a breach of trust and created a huge problem for the couple. Thus, candor can be an incredibly important enhancer—or force multiplier, as we say in the army—of relationship unity.

At its essence, marriage is a union of two people physically, emotionally, and spiritually. There cannot be an important part of your life that is kept secret from your spouse. Couples need more communication, including candor, to succeed, not less time communicating and less honesty. The latter is what gets couples into trouble. With my wife, Lauri, I have learned that I need to share everything with her because, when I don't, little problems become larger problems.

Raising teenagers placed an enormous strain on us because the kids would sometimes unintentionally pit us against the other. We quickly realized that if we were not on the same page as a couple, these parenting challenges could negatively impact the intimacy and trust we have as a couple. With discussion, this issue became easier to resolve; but we had to intentionally spend time discussing it.

Hidden issues that develop over time begin to erode the sacred trust a couple started out with. By spending time together to discuss these issues candidly, often they can be quickly squelched. Your life mate is not your enemy. Many times a lack of trust with your partner is the enemy.

How does candor come into play in marriage? In the diagram below, there is a brick wall between issues and a greater intimacy in marriage. The wall represents hidden issues.

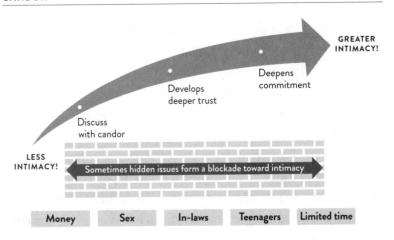

The issues themselves are often not the problem in a marriage because nearly every couple has a host of issues they have to work through. How they deal with the issues can determine success and prevent unresolved problems from becoming hidden issues that eventually form a wall between husband and wife. For instance, every couple deals with in-law issues, such as which day during the holidays to spend with them. Not discussing this openly is how a hidden issue becomes a brick in the wall that causes a lack of intimacy.

By regularly integrating candor into a marriage, the issues can be avenues by which a husband and wife develop deeper trust and a deeper commitment. This is what we all want. I did not marry my spouse to feel alienated from her. Yet, many couples live this way. Deeper intimacy is the goal. The more you discuss concerns with your spouse and are honest with him or her, the stronger your relationship grows.

Candor is the key. Now let's discuss how to implement it.

THE COMMUNICATION ACCELERATOR METHOD

When a couple sits down to discuss things, it can result in a greater sense of frustration and sometimes even a blowup. Some couples quit trying to have deeper discussions altogether to avoid pain. This is heartbreaking because of the intimacy gap that develops. Over time, the couple ceases to know each other and shows little concern or remorse for bad actions.

It is important to have a tool to enhance communication so that it doesn't end in a fight. The tool I use is called the Communication Accelerator Method, or CAM.[2] Here are the basics of CAM:

Step 1: Person #1 begins to speak.

Step 2: Person #2 listens intently and does not interrupt.

Step 3: Person #1 finishes their thought.

Step 4: Before Person #2 responds to what Person #1 has said. They must repeat back—or summarize—what Person #1 has just said.

Step 5: Person #1 clarifies their statement.

Step 6: Person #2 summarizes again until Person #1 is finished or desires a response.

As you can see above, all the attention is focused on what Person #1 has to say. The cycle might need to be repeated so that Person #1 feels fully listened to before continuing on to Step 7 below.

Step 7: Person #2 begins to speak, at this point addressing the issues Person #1 brought up.

Step 8: Person #1 listens intently and does not interrupt.

Step 9: Person #2 finishes their thought.

Step 10: Before Person #1 responds to what Person #2 has said, they must summarize what Person #2 has said.

Step 11: Person #2 clarifies their statement.

Step 12: Person #1 summarizes again until Person #2 is finished or desires a response.

Even in these last six steps, the attention is still on the topic that Person #1 chose. Once all twelve steps are concluded, Person #2 can introduce a new topic of conversation and begin with Step 1. These twelve steps are important for the first speaker to feel fully listened to. Does this feel unduly rigid? Absolutely. However, it is much better than ending a discussion in an argument or an explosion of hate-filled words.

Here is an example of this in a marriage conversation.

Step 1: Kim says, "Greg, I don't feel as if you've been hearing me lately. I need more help around the house, keeping it clean and keeping the laundry going and the clothes folded."

Step 2: Greg's first impulse is to explain how much he is working outside of the home and the time it takes, but he doesn't go there. Instead he keeps listening.

Step 3: Kim explains, "Honey, sometimes I am drained by the end of the night and don't even have the energy to have a conversation with you."

Step 4: Greg summarizes and says, "Honey, you are saying that you would like me to be more attentive at home, unloading the dishwasher, taking out the trash, and helping with the children's bedtime chores instead of watching television. I know I can do more by helping with the supper prep or cleaning dishes or folding laundry."

Step 5: Kim exclaims, "Yes, that is exactly what I am saying. When you take an interest in all the things I have to get done before we enter the bedroom, it makes me want to spend more quality time with you."

Step 6: Greg summarizes and says, "So you don't *want* to be exhausted when we go to bed, it just ends up that way because a lot of the load is on you in the evening."

For steps 7–12, Greg can then explain his side of the story while still keeping to the issue Kim brought up. For instance, Greg might explain how early he wakes up, and how exhausted he is when he arrives home.[3] At this point of the discussion, Kim is listening and repeating back how Greg feels. After he is finished, she then has the opportunity to continue on with that thread of conversation or switch to another topic, perhaps letting Greg go first.

I realize this is not rocket science but can sometimes feel un-wieldy. My wife and I practice this in our home, and over time, we have learned to do it naturally. It is especially hard to continue to listen and not to interject when you feel as if your spouse is saying something inaccurate. But letting them finish their thought allows them to feel validated and listened to. A spouse is much more eager to listen after he or she has been heard.

In this book, we've discussed a lot about listening, especially as it relates to candid feedback. Yes, listening is not the easiest thing to do; in fact, it—is—hard. It does not come naturally for me or for many people. Sometimes we have to train ourselves to listen better, like when we're in college and enrolled in a difficult course. Or when we're with a family member and distractions are competing for our attention. Dutch theologian Henri Nouwen acknowledged the challenge of being a good listener:

> To listen is very hard, because it asks of us so much interior stability that we no longer need to prove ourselves by speeches, arguments, statements, or declarations. True listeners no longer have an inner need to make their presence known. They are free to receive, to welcome, to accept. Listening is much more than allowing another to talk while waiting for a chance to respond. Listening is paying full attention to others and welcoming them into our very beings.[4]

Do you have so much interior stability that you no longer need to prove yourself? Few people would affirm that they do. (We'll explore this in chapter 5.) It is important to capture the essence of what Nouwen is saying about listening: being free to receive, to welcome, to accept. This is at the heart of CAM—not interrupting but allowing your spouse to truly share his or her heart.

In one way, you have already proven yourself to your spouse. They stood before God and everyone accepting you as their soulmate. This sacred act should inspire us to, as Nouwen states, "no longer have an inner need to make our presence known." When fully loved by another, we can fully give ourselves in return. One of the greatest gifts to give is to truly listen to our mate and to connect with their soul.

In addition, we need to continually ask ourselves: "Is it my goal to be right, or is it my goal to preserve the relationship?" If it is the latter, then I can be patient and let my spouse say whatever it is she wants to say. Sometimes I have to check myself because my entire intent is simply to be right, often at the expense of the relationship. But the relationship is ultimate, so if I am sacrificing it for my own ego, that is a terrible position to be in.

Here are some other practical steps to consider when using candor in your marriage.

Don't think "last laugh," think "win-win." Think about how demonstrating candor positively can impact the situation and bring it to a good conclusion. Think in terms of positivity: what is the best case, or most hopeful outcome, for both parties involved? At times, sarcasm and competition exist within marriage. We have to control the feeling that we can get an edge or a higher score. In marriage, no one gains if one loses. Candor is a critical tool in serious marriage discussions because it is about honesty and developing a more trusting relationship. Unfortunately, people lie to their spouse or "shade the truth," which is obviously not a win for anyone.

When unable to reach a conclusive decision, agree to read-dress the topic later. A healthy pause might be more helpful to the relationship than a personal win. One person might need time to process things more clearly. My spouse is a quick thinker and can process items as they are spoken; I take more time to process what has been said. Injecting candor usually speeds up discussion processes because you no longer have to guess what someone else is thinking. However, there may be times that even with candor present, it is best to stop the discussion and agree to readdress the topic later. You do not want a rushed decision if not everyone is on board with all the components.

Speak to your spouse in private about something that troubles you. When you do not agree with your spouse, or when you feel the urge to criticize them, this is received much better in a private setting rather than around friends, family (including your children), or work associates. Many marriages have suffered over comments made in a public setting where the reputation of one of the spouses is diminished. This is not a departure from candor, but it follows the candor principle outlined in the first chapter: candor is to be done in love and at an appropriate time to help. When that time comes and you are alone, be courageous and bring up the hard topics. Explain to your spouse what, if anything, irritates you. Own how you might be irritating to others. Be as honest as possible when you're alone instead of throwing truth fastballs in public.

What do we have to gain from embarrassing our spouse in a public setting? If what you have to say has the potential to upset your spouse, then it is much better to speak those words in private. If communicated in public, what are your spouse's options? They can retaliate or yell at you, but that quickly becomes uncomfortable for everyone else too. In private, it is possible to use CAM and resolve issues respectfully.

● ● ●

Romance and sexual intimacy with our spouses can be the hardest topics to discuss. Candor is *crucial* here.

● ● ●

Avoid superlatives, "I always" or "you never." This is a must for healthy relationships. A situation may seem to warrant using a superlative, but if you stop to think about it, many times emotions are simply having their way with your words. Few people *always* act in a way that might be bothersome to you. In my marriage, I have learned to stop and address my wife's feelings in the honesty of the moment. It can take courage to inject candor at these points because I may not like the answer. For instance, I might ask, "Do you truly believe I *always* act this way?" If that is indeed her impression, then I need to think about my actions.

There is one parting consideration before we leave this marriage section—sex. Romance and sexual intimacy with our spouses can be the hardest topics to discuss. Candor is *crucial* here. It is impossible to know what another is thinking, especially in the middle of the night when one or both people might be exhausted. Some of the hardest words to say are, "Honey, I want to talk with you about our sex life." Even one person speaking up, however, can keep one or both from hours of nervous wrangling on this subject. A little candor from either the husband or the wife can quickly open the door to greater sexual intimacy.

Here is an example of forthright honesty and truth, given in a loving way, when needed, to benefit your lover. "Honey, I am not feeling 100 percent right now. What if we planned for time together tomorrow afternoon on our day off?" This little statement can save many moments of stress and anxiety in the bedroom. It is not saying "no," or "later," and gives both people something to look forward to the next day.

Candor is about intimacy, so there is no greater place for it than in this wonderful and intimate aspect of married life. Developing a deeper union—emotionally, spiritually, and physically—is what marriage is about. A commitment statement for this section might be: I am committed to this relationship, therefore I will give and receive candor.

CANDOR IN PARENTING

Much of what we've covered about candor in marriage can also be applied to raising children. Obviously, depending on their age, we have to tailor some of the skills to be effectively used with kids. However, when my children were teenagers they were fully capable of using CAM and wanted to on occasion. It was exciting for them to get the floor and be allowed to speak without someone interrupting them. I learned as a parent that we sometimes do not give our kids the same respect as we would another person's child or even a stranger. We find it okay to cut them off or belittle them in front of others, which is always wrong.

So how does CAM work with kids? Very well. When Lauri and I have something serious we want to speak to our children about, we first set up a time to discuss it with them.

There are additional steps in the process to accommodate children:

1. Set up a time to talk. Sometimes the supper table is not best if others are present.

2. Introduce them to the CAM technique.

3. Explain your position to them.

4. Allow them to summarize what you have told them.

5. Then listen—truly listen—to their response.

6. Set ground rules for future behavior.

Sometimes children are quiet and it seems like we have to pry things out of our children. When I ask my child how school was and they reply, "fine," that is not good enough for me. "Okay, what was fine about it? Did everything go well with your teachers today? Are you getting along with other students? How was practice after school? Do you have any plans for the weekend? How are your grades?"

Using candor to ask good questions is essential in parenting. A lot of kids don't freely offer up much information, unless they are the talkative type. Over time, I have forgotten how hard it was to go to junior high school. Adolescence can be brutal. Sometime kids will nobly try to shelter their parents from how tough things are going for them. This is where candor comes in. We continually have to work at building bridges so that we can receive candor and have others want to give candor to us. I *want* to know what is going on in my kid's heart, and I *want* them to want to share it with me. That doesn't mean I force them to speak if they don't want to. Kids will shut down when overpressed.

The information from the leader section in chapter 3 can actually be applied to receiving candor from your kids.

Receiving Candor
1. Be patient
2. Listen attentively with an open mind
3. Embrace the discomfort
4. Be appreciative
5. Believe the best of the speaker and their motives

Patience with children is terribly important. We might try to speak to our kids and get rebuffed nine times out of ten. But it is that tenth time when we can make some real inroads with building trust and deepening the relationship. Once kids speak up, we have to resist the temptation to interrupt them or correct them. Kids can be inconsistent and not have good justifications for their arguments. As parents who have lived full lives, we can easily spot inconsistencies in rationale. While it seems important at the time to correct their words, this can cripple communication. Kids do not want to be interrupted or corrected any more than we do. Once they start talking, be patient, let them tell their story, question some things after they have finished, and be appreciative and supportive.

There are certain axiomatic truths that I figured everyone knew, but some folks are downright rude or impatient with their kids. C. S. Lewis speaks about this issue in *The Four Loves*. He states that some parents routinely treat their children rudely in public settings, and then cannot understand why the children are never at home. Perhaps it is because they "prefer civility to barbarism," Lewis explains.[5] Respect works both ways. We expect our children to respect us; we should also respect them. Part of how to do this is to give candor to them and receive candor from them. We may think we know our kids so well that we don't need to truly listen to them, but this is not true.

For maximum impact with kids it is important to work through bad moods—both yours and your child's—and speak to the issue while it is on the table. This means we must be in the moment, listening attentively, and asking our children to repeat something if it does not sound quite right. This will provide time to take a deep breath and think while they are talking. When our kids are ready to speak, it is much easier for them to trust us and to speak with candor if we aren't prying things out of them. Be in the moment. Engage when you can. Strike when the iron is hot. Often, when things get put off, they can be forgotten and not dealt with in a timely way. And sometimes the bad mood is related to what my child may or may not be thinking about the situation at hand. When it is resolved, their bad mood sometimes goes away.

If children become irrational or out of control, it is more important than ever to deliver forthright honesty, no matter how they may try to reshape it. As the parent, with candor, you are able to bring reality to the situation. For instance, you may have a child who has a bad habit or an addiction and continually tries to justify this detrimental behavior. One cannot be complicit with this shading and changing the truth. You are your child's most important authority figure. Speaking up with candor and expressing not only how you feel about it, but also explaining why the behavior is harmful is important. Our children need us to be truth-tellers. Empathy is not enough.

CANDOR WITH PARENTS AND IN-LAWS

For a final note on candor in families, let's address dealing with our families of origin. Not all of us have ideal situations with our parents. Our parents or stepparents can be quick to criticize; they can be unforgiving or downright rude to us, our spouses, and our children. Strained relationships with in-laws can be incredibly painful to deal with and navigate, especially during the holidays. I do not presume that speaking with candor will solve decades-old personality flaws or long ago trauma. Healthy boundaries are important. What I do recommend is that when it comes to us, candor can help dismantle ancient walls.

There are so many complex feelings and emotions wrapped up in relating to our parents, but candor is crucial here as well. Some couples have had to relate to in-laws who have totally different values than the ones they want to instill in their own family. Some of us have aging parents, now perhaps remarried, where normal discussions about finances and the future take on a whole new meaning.

To provide an example of this in an effort to show how candor might be used with the older generation, here is a conversation that I had to have once with my dad.

Me: "Hey, Dad, I need to address something with you that is not easy."

My dad: "Yes, what is it?"

Me: "It is your estate. Everything is in a joint account with your wife. Your health is not that good. Is it your intent that if you pass away first that all that you and mom accumulated would go to your new wife's side of the family?"

My dad: "I am not going to pass away first. It is your stepmother who is always ill."

Me: "I know, you have said that a lot, Dad, but I want to make sure that your intentions are met with your estate in case anything happens to your good health. Are you sure that you and your wife should not put everything into a living trust so that all of your heirs are protected?"

My dad: "Is it really that important to you and your siblings to do this?"

Me: "Yes, but not for the reason you may think. We want your intentions to be met. A living trust could be honorable to both sides of the family, and your wife's children can participate in the decision-making."

My dad: "It would be okay with you and your brothers and sister if we split things evenly with my wife's side of the family?"

Me: "Yes, dad. That is what I am saying. We think that this will be the fairest for all parties involved, no matter who may pass away first."

This is just a snippet of the actual conversation. Soon after the conversation my father and my stepmother agreed to a living trust where their assets would be divided equally amongst both sides of the families. A few months later my dad developed severe dementia and would not have been able to have that conversation. Three years later, he passed away. My siblings point back to the conversation that I had with my dad as a significant turning point in his financial decisions.

It was equitable and caring for him to develop a living trust, but it was not an easy conversation to have. My dad could have questioned my motives. He could have refused to discuss his finances with his youngest child. But he didn't. Both of us gave and received candor in the conversation, and it was helpful to the entire family, including his stepchildren, who have blessed us with their hospitality.

Some parents will not be open to financial or other personal conversations with their kids. It can be hard for them to think about the future. There were additional discussions with my dad about losing his driver's license, moving to a smaller home, and moving into a care facility. Some of the conversations he did not like. But they were real issues and they needed to be addressed. I am thankful that I am in a loving family where my brothers and sister respect and honor each other.

An acquaintance named Cynthia explained to me she used candor with her father at their Christmas holiday gathering. She deliberated quite a while, but then told her dad that it would mean a lot to her if he attended Christmas Eve service with her family. He spoke for a while about his own views of life and why he did not attend church, but eventually he consented. Cynthia was thankful she had used courage to speak to her father about something important to her. Her candor provided this opportunity to spend time with her father in a meaningful setting, and her father ended up being glad she asked.

I hope you find candor to be helpful in your relationships with your spouse, your children, and your parents.

SUMMARY

Speaking with candor to those we love might involve some of the hardest conversations we ever have. With our spouses, it is absolutely critical to be honest with each other. We do not have to see eye-to-eye on everything—that would be impossible. But in order to fully share life with each other, we must speak with honesty, love, and an intention for their betterment . . . the building blocks of true candor. With our children, it is important not to criticize them unnecessarily, to respect their opinions, and listen to them as we would other adults and children. Using candor and the communication acceleration method (CAM) can help with all our relationships, especially those whom we are deeply committed to.

Strategies for Families

1. Don't think "last laugh," think "win-win." Think about how demonstrating candor positively can impact the situation and bring it to a good conclusion.

2. When unable to reach a conclusive decision, agree to readdress the topic later. A healthy pause might be more helpful to the relationship than a personal win.

3. Speak to your spouse in private, if possible, especially if the subject matter is sensitive in nature and can be brokered without a group discussion.

4. Avoid superlatives such as "you always" or "I never."

5. For maximum impact with kids, it is important to work through bad moods and speak to the issue while it is on the table. This means your bad moods and your child's bad moods. It means we must be in the moment, listening attentively, and asking our children to repeat something if it does not sound quite right. This will provide time to take a deep breath and think while they are talking.

Reflection Questions

1. How are your current listening skills? Do you believe that when you listen, you are free to receive, to accept, or to reject based on what is being said?

2. Are you able to be humble around your kids and truly listen to them?

3. In your own words, why do you think it is important not to automatically question someone's integrity?

4. Try out CAM with someone in your family. How did it go? Did it make the discussion easier or somewhat awkward? If awkward, don't give up. This structure can assist with difficult conversations.

CANDOR COMMITMENT

I commit to treating people in my family with dignity and respect. All of my relationships are important, but especially those whom I am committed to love. I promise to speak to them with candor!

CHAPTER 5

BLISTERING HONESTY with SELF

You've got to be yourself. You've got to be comfortable in your shoes. . . . People can see through a phony in a minute.[1]

—JACK WELCH

How are you doing?

When people ask you this question, how do you usually respond? Most of us respond with the typical "fine." This chapter is about looking a little deeper into who we are and how we operate.

During counseling sessions, I have tested many hundreds, possibly thousands, of people with either temperament sorters[2] or with the Words and Deeds Integrity Assessment tool I created in 2016.[3] One thing I have learned is that people will sometimes answer questions based on who they *want* to be, rather than who they truly are. There is a mental game some play when assessing themselves, hoping to come out as a certain type of person. I am not sure about all the factors that drive this behavior, but I always caution people before an assessment to answer as honestly as possible, not who they want to be but who they truly are inside.

The benefits of people being honest with themselves is that they can gain a clear picture of who they are, and then use it as a baseline for where they want to go and who they want to be. Without this baseline, any gain is suspect. There would always be a question of whether an individual is truly advancing or possibly going backwards. We could never know where someone might be if they don't tell the truth on assessments.

> **People sometimes answer questions based on who they *want* to be, rather than who they truly are.**

This lack of self-veracity phenomenon leads to the question: is candor easier with others or with ourselves? Societal candor appears to be easier to express with other people than with ourselves. As a reminder, societal candor is typically rooted in pride and involves bullying and bitterness. What we communicate is filtered through these actions and traits and outward to others. But it is the opposite with true candor. We must have true candor with ourselves before we can have it with others.

The very essence of true candor is that it is an intentional act of love toward others. Typically, initiating love comes from people who know themselves and are comfortable in their own skin. It is honesty, objectivity, self-awareness, and an understanding that our lives are a mixture of both faults and strengths. Over time, as true candor with "self" grows, a person better develops skills of giving and receiving candor. There is a similar courage needed for both true candor with others and candor with ourselves.

In the previous four chapters, we have learned about giving and receiving candor with other people at work and at home. Now it is time to focus on ourselves. We'll start with two questions:

1. First, have you ever listened to yourself thinking?

2. Second, if after listening to yourself thinking, have you ever changed your course of direction because of the process of actively tuning in?

I know these may sound like odd questions to ask, but they are important ones. When we start listening to ourselves thinking, we begin to identify a lot more about ourselves. For instance, I can think something like the following: "Why did I get up late this morning? Now I'm running around like crazy and will be late for work." This type of thought runs through our head most of the time without us truly considering it. We don't because we already know the answer and we don't want to deal with the change it might require.

For instance, in this leaving-late scenario, it could be assumed that I stayed up too late, a conscious decision I made the night before. Or, I hit the snooze button too many times when the alarm went off. As I question myself, I know the answer to my own questions, but I don't take time to think about them and make a change. It is easier just to grumble to myself and to not ever take any action. Listening to our thought process is imperative if we're going to, in turn, give candor to ourselves and experience true growth and contentment.

Life success seminars motivate people to take some action that moves their lives in the right direction. Some seminars focus more on future behavior. They operate on the premise that, to be successful, it doesn't matter what has happened in the past, you only need to imagine who you are going to be in the future. Another life success theory deals with all the serious issues in the past so you can move forward and not have these issues bother you anymore. I'm not minimizing those who are trying to help other people, or the value of personality and integrity assessments; however, being honest with ourselves about where we are right now is usually the most beneficial way toward helping people in the long run.[4]

We can practice the skills of giving and receiving candor, but at some point we have to look in the mirror and figure out who we are, what we are saying and doing, and how this is impacting us. Then, and only then, can we decide if we are doing the right things in the right way. Many of us are wearing masks to portray a false self. This must be dealt with first.

THE FALSE SELF

Scientists tell us we have certain inherent needs as humans that we are born with, and that these needs grow in us as we become adults. One of the needs is to belong, like to a family or to meaningful institutions. Another need is accomplishment, and/or some sense of making progress. An additional need is to have purpose and another is to love. When we do not have "wins" in these areas, we end up putting on masks to make it seem to the outside world as if we are actually doing fine. We wrongly think that if our true self is too "ugly" to display to the public, then we must change the narrative so that people will still like us.

What I have found in life is that the opposite is usually true: when I am honest with people about how I am *really* doing, then they accept me more and welcome me into their confidence. When I am more authentic with others—though it exposes my flaws—I become more cherished and relatable. It is counterintuitive. When I am more transparent, people are not repulsed; they feel more connected to me because they've experienced similar issues in their own lives.

Why would someone willingly wear a mask? The basic needs of life are to belong, to have purpose and find success, and to be loved. When we don't feel these things, we learn to fake it. This is the false self.

Psychologist David G. Benner speaks to this challenge of authenticity. In his book, *The Gift of Being Yourself*, he states:

At some point in childhood we all make the powerful discovery that we can manipulate the truth about ourselves. Initially it often takes the form of a simple lie—frequently a denial of having done something. But of more importance to the development of the false self is the discovery that our ability to hide isn't limited to what we say or don't say. We learn to pretend. We discover the art of packaging our self.

We learn that even if we feel afraid, we can appear to be brave. We also learn to cloak hate with apparent love, anger with apparent calm, and indifference with apparent sympathy. In short, we learn how to present our self in the best possible light—a light designed to create a favorable impression and maintain our self-esteem.[5]

As Benner explains, the false self is about pretending so that we can be seen in the best possible light and so that others will admire us more. Is it really that important for others to think so highly of us? For some, this façade means *everything* to them and must never be cracked open because the real self may let people down.

Many of us have learned how to fake it around others. We have learned to pretend. We form an identity we present to others that we know is not really our true self. There is dissonance between who people think we are and who we actually are. We care more about maintaining an image than nurturing our real identity. That's why it is irritating when people see through us; the masks we have so carefully created are in jeopardy of forming cracks which others can see through.

Unfortunately, as a younger man, I was not good at practicing candor with myself.

I had fallen into a rhythm of comparing myself to those around me, trying to outdo others and—in the most awkward attempt of all—trying to appear humble about my achievements, a mask I would use over and over again when it suited me. I struggled with my identity and other issues for a long time. Even as a young army chaplain, I did not rightly consider or perceive that God and other people could love me for who I actually was. I wrongly thought that the false self I was presenting to others would lead to a greater sense of joy and fulfillment.

What I failed to appreciate is this: not only did people like the real me and respond better when I was authentic, but they preferred the real me. They preferred me with all my flaws, rather than the carefully painted portrait of who I wanted to be. Turned out, I was not as clever as I thought in deceiving others. I learned that honesty was the most important ingredient when it came to relationships, not self-preservation and reputation management.

What are some of the false masks that you wear? Do you feel the need to routinely try to present to others the best scenario of your life as possible? Are you trying to show yourself as someone more successful? Are you trying to communicate to others that you have a certain level of contentment, when deep down you know that is not true?

Can you picture yourself being your authentic, transparent self around others and having them love and respect you more deeply because of it? Can you picture not wearing any masks? We all know what it feels like to be around those who are name-droppers and one-uppers. It makes us feel small. Yet, when we are around those who are comfortable with themselves, freely sharing their mistakes or struggles, it encourages us as fellow human beings who sometimes may be struggling to make it through the day.

Now, there are limits to this, of course. For instance, depending on the context and the people present, it is not wise to share faults or to do so in order to win friends. However, with a simple act of being more honest and transparent about myself, I'm better able to empathize with others in their situations and respond with understanding and compassion.

CANDOR WITH SELF

So how do we get there? Self-candor has a lot to do with it, and completing a simple survey on areas of your life can assist with this. As this chapter is titled "Blistering Honesty with Self," this section contains a series of questions that will help you identify areas in which you may need to have more honesty and, by doing so, experience more satisfaction and joy.

Here is the first series:

1. What are the issues in your life that you are not happy with?
2. Are you facing them squarely, or refusing to acknowledge them?
3. For instance, are you constantly late, constantly changing diets, constantly changing relationships, or constantly changing jobs?
4. Are you content with where you are or would you say you are more discontent?

Sometimes we do not take the time to acknowledge items in our lives that are troubling us, and they eventually manifest themselves in ways that may seem odd to those around us. Take Kenny from chapter 2, for instance. He struggles with relationships, and although this is a constant issue in his life, he refuses to acknowledge it. Some might think he never will, that it is futile to try to change people. However, there are small steps anyone can take with self-candor that can have a big impact.

The first step is listening to what you're thinking. What goes on in the mind is an amazing thing. When we listen to ourselves and hear ourselves saying that this or that person doesn't like us, we need to confront these thoughts with candor. We can ask ourselves, *Am I sure about that? What proof do I have?* Perhaps people are not thinking about us as much as we think they are. Perhaps they are simply trying to make it through their day and similarly concerned with what people think about them.

Stop and think about some recent interactions you have had with others. What was going on in your mind? Were you thinking about how you could impress them? Were you wondering what they think about you? Were you disappointed that you were not making a better impression on them? When we listen in and hear ourselves thinking that we need to impress the person next to us, with some timely self-candor we can quickly confront the thought and ask *why* we think it. Do we want to impress that person because they are wealthy? Popular? Liked by important people who I want to like me?

The second step is to figure out what you want in life. Some may feel disconnected from their purpose. Here are some simple steps that can help connect you with your goals by using candor with yourself and others:

1. Figure out what type of person you want to be (strong, kind, genuine).
2. Know what you want in life (goals, passions).
3. Communicate what you want to others.
4. Believe in yourself when you hit roadblocks.

Addressing the areas above may not result in immediate success, but the peace of mind it brings will smooth the path toward success. These are areas that help us develop a certain amount of emotional maturity. When we truly want to improve as people, we can also consider the following questions (with the subsequent information), asking them of yourself, and answering each of them truthfully:

What are others commenting about your behavior, and is there any truth to what they are saying?

At times, we don't hear what others are saying, especially if it is something negative about us. We have to take a strategic pause and really listen so we can understand the feedback that's being given. I have learned that when feedback irritates me, it is usually because there is some truth to it, and it stresses me out that others might know me so well.

Are you making adjustments based on those acknowledgments?

Are you applying what you are learning about yourself? Take the earlier "waking up late" scenario. If I truly think about it and understand why I am hurrying around in the morning, I need to ask if I am frustrated enough to change this behavior or not. If I am, and I think about it rationally, then I can decide to change it. And it is easy: I begin by not hitting the snooze so often. Living in a world where we do not have to acknowledge what we are thinking may be simple in the short run, but it is not a formula for success. Having a firm grasp of reality will not only help us with internal deliberations, it will also help us identify if we are wearing masks around others.

We need to be in a regular habit of taking time to see how we are doing and asking ourselves specific questions. (We'll do this in the Self-Candor Exercise.)

The process you use with self-candor follows the same steps for giving candor to others. Try practicing these four steps with yourself.

Giving Candor
1. Speak the unspoken truth
2. With love
3. When needed
4. To benefit ourselves

Do you ask yourself the tough questions? Do you care about yourself enough to try to make a positive difference in your life? Just like when receiving candor from others, you need to be patient with the process. Also, some of the answers you come up with might feel a little uncomfortable, but that is okay. Embrace the discomfort. It is truth and honesty we are after. The more self-candor, the more truth. The more truth, the more growth. And growth is the goal. The more growth, the more wholesome, life-sustaining relationships we will experience. This means more joy for us and those in relationship with us.

As a practical exercise, here are some questions to ask yourself. The first ten questions focus on inner joy and contentment. The next ten questions focus on how you engage with those around you. It is the first ten areas that drive the answers in the second ten areas.

Self-Candor Exercise

1. Am I content with my life right now?
2. Am I happy with the direction I am going?
3. Do I belong to a meaningful organization?
4. Am I contributing in a positive way to society?
5. Am I in meaningful relationships?
6. Do I contribute to my relationships in a positive way and for the betterment of others?
7. Have I been successful with my life so far?
8. Do I have a sense of purpose?
9. Do I look forward to the future?
10. Do I feel ashamed in any of the areas listed in the above questions?
11. Can I be completely open and honest with those around me?
12. Am I vulnerable and transparent in my closest relationships?
13. Am I presenting a false self to others?
14. Do I feel the tendency to wear masks around others?

15. Are there things I hide from others?
16. Am I afraid of something in my life coming out into the open?
17. Are there things in my life I am choosing not to deal with?
18. Are there things in my life I need to change or get rid of?
19. Do I feel the need to impress others?
20. Do I worry about or am I overly concerned with what people think about me?

Let's unpack a few of the questions. The first ten questions survey different aspects of your life. Some people don't ever pause to think about these items. For instance, question #6 is: *Do I contribute to my relationships in a positive way and for the betterment of others?* How do you go about answering a question like this? First, you might think about some of the relationships in your life right now among coworkers, neighbors, and family. Consider if lately you have been more of a taker or more of a giver, and also if people are receiving you well or avoiding you. The goal is to continue to contribute to your relationships in a positive way.

Some sub-questions that could be asked for #6 are: *Am I being intentional about reaching out to others, even those I disagree with, or don't really enjoy spending time with? Do I feel the need to constantly explain myself to others, or am I more a listening ear for those who need to talk? Do I think people are energized after being around me, or do they walk away feeling burdened?* You may not know the answer to all of these, but the important thing is that you are considering these ideas and taking the time for introspection and self-awareness—this process never hurt anyone and usually brings greater joy and self-contentment when acted upon.

Now let's focus on a couple of questions from the second set: #12, *Am I vulnerable and transparent in my closest relationships?* To answer this question, you may want to ask someone who is close to you if they find you vulnerable. What does it mean to be vulnerable? There are several definitions, such as being open to harm. In the context of candor, vulnerability means letting your guard down, being honest with your real feelings, and not trying to cover up anything. Here's an example. About twelve years ago, I was assessed by people who described me as being closed off and hard to get to know. I have grown in this area by applying the principles of candor. Vulnerability can become the gateway to honesty, transparency, and closeness.

Now let's look at #14: *Do I feel the tendency to wear masks around others?* This is another tough question. There is a fine line between performing in a role and wearing a mask. When we work in our vocation, we are considered to be professionals in the jobs we do. We must *present* ourselves to be proficient and knowledgeable in our work. Who wouldn't want to hire someone competent and confident in their career field? However, where the mask comes into play is when we feel that we have to know all the answers, that there cannot be a dent in our armor, that we must be the best in our profession.

This push for being the best and brightest (the star of the company, the smartest person in the room) or to always need to have your opinion heard and to shape your environment so that you are seen as special, might be indicative of wearing a mask and not being honest about who you truly are. These attempts masquerade as pathways to personal freedom; but they, in fact, limit us and turn out to be a cage. The less candid we are with ourselves and others, the more we limit true expression that is freely given and warmly received.

THE END GOAL—SELF AWARENESS

Self-awareness means being comfortable in our own skin and not wearing masks. At some point in our lives, we have to come to a place where we acknowledge that what we do and say has an impact on everyone else in the room. Before I can have candor with others in a dynamic and ever-changing society, some soul-searching is required to see what I actually do believe. And in this practice of self-candor, we must be intentional; passivity in a roaring river takes you miles downstream.

SUMMARY

Candor with ourselves can be a challenge. Our tendency may be to present to the world a portrait of how we are doing that is far from reality. The reasons that drive this are many. Being honest with our own lives and our inner conversations can lead to tremendous healing and growth. The notion that people will like us better if we have it all together is a myth. The more honest we are and the more authentic to our true self, the more doors open to deep friendships and healed family relationships. People are waiting to see the real you, but for this to happen, you have to initiate self-candor and take action.

Reflection questions

1. What are you most afraid of in life? How does this answer impact your everyday behavior?

2. What are some of the false masks you wear, i.e. allowing others to see a certain persona of you that is not entirely true?

3. Are you currently in reputation management mode, or do you believe people are experiencing the real you?

4. Take some time and ask yourself the twenty questions in this chapter. Provide ultra-honest answers to yourself, and write them down. If comfortable, show them to a person who knows you well and receive their perspective about some of your answers.

CANDOR COMMITMENT

I commit to using candor with myself by asking tough questions, seeking honest answers, and being observant and reflective in regard to what others are saying about my behavior. Instead of wearing a mask, I want to be in touch with how I am really doing so I can be honest with myself and other people, and thus reach the goal of self-awareness.

CHAPTER 6

The INDISPENSABLE FRIENDSHIP FACTOR

Candor is a compliment, it implies equality; it's how true friends talk.[1]

—PEGGY NOONAN

Now that we have dealt with self, we are in a great position to progress and use candor with those we enjoy free time with—our friends. What is a friend? My personal definition is: someone I can let my guard down with, I am energized by being with, and I can be transparent with. He or she is someone whose opinion I can trust. They stick with you through poverty and plenty. You may not hear from a true friend for a long time, but when you reconnect, it is as if you never separated. When a group of some type gathers—say, at a park—the closest friends are those who walk side-by-side while the main group goes on ahead, just so that they can eke out a little more time together to catch up. These two will stay friends even when the main group loses touch.

At its essence, friendship looks like this: friends tell friends the truth. A friend is one who is honest with you, so candor is the ultimate distinguisher of whether a person is a true friend or not. Surface friendships cannot tolerate candor; true friendships thrive on it. Surface friendships stick to the easy subjects; true friendships thrive on discussing religion and politics and laughing at each other's quirks. Candor is an instrument, or sword, which reveals what kind of friend a person truly is because it cuts through surface issues.

Think for a moment about some of the people in your life right now. Who are those who you believe you will stay close with even if you don't communicate regularly? Who are those you will cease communication with once time moves on? There is a difference between having a surface friend and having a true friend. Injecting candor into a relationship for any length of time allows for the possibility of a lifelong friend and trusted companion.

Recall the quad diagram in the first chapter:

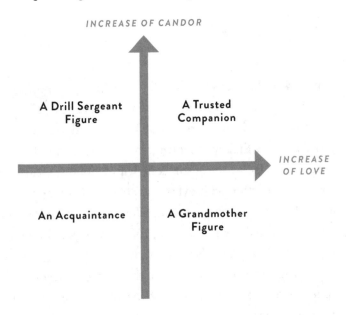

With an increase of love but decrease in candor, you have a grandmother figure, i.e., those who care about you but do not challenge you. It is *friends* in your life—trusted companions—who balance both candor and love in their relationship with you. Don't get me wrong, sometimes we need only love. That is what family is for, to love us unconditionally no matter what we may say or do. But with true friendship, familiarity does not blind us to another's faults. We choose our friends, and they choose us. We can move on if so desired, and people can move away from us. We are not stuck with friends. Friends are the extras in life, relationships that bring much joy and little sacrifice. In the diagram above, those high in love and candor are labeled as "Trusted Companions."

Think for a minute about a time when you thought a friend was rude to you but then later realized they were helping out of love. There is a story that illustrates this about a goose, a cow, and a cat.[2] During the year's southern migration, one goose was having a hard time staying in the V formation and ended up veering off from his friends. He eventually crashed through the roof of an old barn. He landed, dazed, in the straw next to a large cow. The startled goose began to regain his composure when all of a sudden the cow dumped a coating of manure all over the unfortunate fowl. It was a terrible experience but the goose realized it actually protected him from the evening chill. Suddenly, a cat jumped through a barn window and went straight for the goose. The manure-covered goose was about to flee, but the cat approached slowly, then took a lot of time to lick off the goose, which the goose appreciated. Once the cat finished cleaning the goose, she ate him. The moral of the story is: not everyone who dumps on you is your enemy, and not everyone who helps you out is your friend.

Sometimes there are people in our lives who are extra kind, or attempt to go out of their way to help us, when all along they have an ulterior motive, or want to use their relationship with us for their own personal gain. Initially, they appear to be a friend, but then they let us down. Other times, we have people in our lives who talk straight to us and some of their words might hurt. We might believe they have gone too far or they are getting too personal. Yet, when the words are truthful and for our good, this is the language of trusted friends.

There are two verses from the Bible that explain this. The first is, "As iron sharpens iron, so one person sharpens another."[3] The second is, "If the axe is dull and the blade unsharpened, more strength must be exerted."[4] True friendships sharpen us so we are all-around better people, more effective at communicating, and more relatable. Without the honesty of true friends, our lives would be harder because we would have less self-awareness. Trusted companions help us in many ways, and not solely by loving us, but by using abundant candor.

When both people in a friendship use candor, an alchemy happens, bonding them for a lifetime. Please notice the evolution from the first graph above into the modified graphs below.

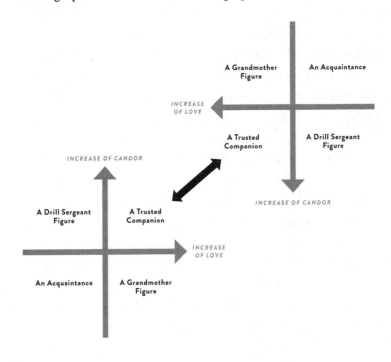

As both friends use an abundance of love and candor with each other, each becomes a trusted—or true—companion of the other, doubling the strength of the relationship.

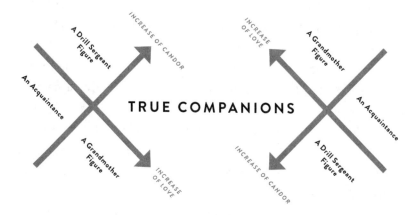

As illustrated, this pact creates the closeness we long for in the journey we call life, a cementing or forging of two people into an intangible reality we call friendship. Without candor and love, these kinds of deep relationships elude us. With candor and love, all things are possible.

Why is candor so important in friendships? Candor is a representation of love for others through our words. Do you have true friends in your life who can tell you when you have spinach in your teeth? Do you have someone who can give you the bare naked truth? Someone who can tell you that you are not speaking kindly to a spouse or child, and can do so in a way that does not destroy your friendship? Have you let others have that kind of candor in your life? Just as leaders do, one has to be in a position to receive candor without feeling threatened.

I am not speaking here about an acquaintance, sibling, or stranger telling you the truth about yourself in an unloving manner, almost as if to punish you. Remember, true candor has no strings attached; it is speaking the unspoken truth, in a loving way, at the appropriate time, for the good of those who hear. That is what makes candor so special between friends: it builds, not ruins, loving relationships. The more candor, the more intimacy. This is important to remember when your true friend says something to you about yourself that you don't like or appreciate at the moment. Remember the goose: not everyone who dumps on you is your enemy.

One evening, I was with a group of colleagues from around the country. We had just completed a seven-week, in-resident course. On the last night, we went out to a restaurant to celebrate. Toward the end of the meal, I offered up to the group that since we would likely never see each other again, we should tell each other our worst flaws, so that we could improve ourselves for the sake of those with whom we worked every day.

The six-person group agreed and around the table we went. Some truly honest feedback was given to each person in a somewhat loving manner, and things were lively and fun . . . until it was my turn. I was leading the conversation, so we focused on me last. In the moments prior, I had come up with a lot of—what I considered—good ideas for others; but when the tables were turned, it was not so fun. The group formed a consensus, and then let me have it about something very true in my life. The feedback was also relevant because that day I had exhibited the very traits they said were a downer to the group dynamic.

Wow, I decided that if I ever had a good idea again, I would give it much more thought before sharing it. I am not sure if the others went home doing as much soul-searching as I did; but needless to say, the exercise worked, and I believe I changed and grew because of it. Many times I thought of the exchange and tried to readjust my behavior. A few years later, I attended an event and ended up running into one of those men. The first thing he said when he saw me was, "Causey! You said we would never see each other again!" We both laughed about that prior experience, and today we are better people because of it and remain good friends. The experiment worked.

PRACTICAL WAYS TO USE CANDOR WITH FRIENDS

When is the right time to use candor with your friends? When you see them straying off course. When they are not living the life you know they want, their best life. When they begin to shade the truth, or say things they don't really mean. These are all times when a healthy dose of candor can be helpful to provide a friend.

With a friend, you have an opportunity to use candor that is not always there with people you work with professionally, or someone who is in your family. You can usually share the truth, knowing there is a high degree of trust, little risk of losing the relationship, and high reward. However, it is important to follow the rules of candor and speak out of your love for them, not simply because of a temporary annoyance you may be feeling.

One of the challenges to know before confronting a friend with candor is if they view your relationship as close and/or as intimate as you do. Try to gauge not only the strength of the friendship from your side of it, but from their perspective as well. You can gain clues from what they are telling you about how they feel about you. At what level of intimacy and trust have they shared information with you?

One way to help deepen a friendship through candor is to put yourself out there first and be vulnerable. You can ask another person the following questions:

1. What is my greatest flaw?
2. What is something I do that gets on your nerves?
3. What is one thing about me that you would change if you could?
4. If you could have another person just like me as a friend, what would you keep out of my personality to make it more enjoyable for you?

I realize that these questions are fairly similar, but in different ways and in a very short time they get to the heart of the matter. Warning: before you ask these questions, you have to be willing to hear honest answers. You have to accept the truth your friends might tell you. You might have to bite your lip before speaking and think the best of them, then take a good look in the mirror following the session before responding.

Our natural desire is to reject feedback about us that seems unpleasant. This is abundantly clear to me whenever I administer personality assessments. For twenty years, I have tested people and provided a four-page personality analysis that includes a section on strengths and a section on weaknesses. In nearly every seminar I teach using this tool, people tell me the assessment is spot on, 99.9 percent, except for one or two little things. Can you guess what they are? A couple of their weaknesses. I have never had one person tell me that the assessment is accurate except for a few of their strengths. This is a psychological phenomenon we all possess and have to work through.

Condemnation of others comes more naturally than exoneration.

Here's an example: when we commit a traffic violation or break a societal rule, we are quick to provide contextual rationale, e.g. I was running late, I've had a tough day, I couldn't see that car because it was in my blind spot. When others are in error, we are not as quick to provide reasons that could exonerate their behavior. *She is always late. He is in another one of his bad moods. That person is a horrible driver, switching lanes like that.*

In essence, we do not instinctively give others the benefit of the doubt as often as we do ourselves. Remember, we judge ourselves by our motives, but we judge others by their behavior; and condemnation of others comes more naturally than exoneration.

For some reason it is easy to excuse our own behavior and hard to excuse others' behavior. We have an internal prejudice that is not present with our own actions. And what's worse, most of us possess a degree of self-verification: wanting others to see us and treat us the way we view ourselves. And this is why candor with friends is so important. It is the looking glass. It fights against forces inside of us that we sometimes don't even realize exist. Candor counters our tendency to self-rationalize and perpetuate unending positive self-attribution. Friends that can help us with this are true friends, indeed.

MAGNANIMITY AND FORGIVENESS

A true friend is:

1. One who is willing to be honest with us, and,
2. One from whom we are willing to receive honest feedback

When these two factors are present, the camouflage discussed in chapter 1 begins to fade away, the real you is exposed, and, in the process, the realness of your friend is exposed as well. Many suffer with the desire to cover over and hide their flaws. This is a natural tendency but doesn't help us in the long run. The more we see the true person we are and the actual state of things, the more easily we can change for the better.

Candor sheds light on a subject. True statements are made. True opinions come out. True feelings are expressed. We move closer to the *realness* of the matter. We become real. We understand that we are real. We sense more that this life means something; we are not just memes and talking heads on a social media platform.

Candor is the indispensable friendship factor because it removes the camouflage clothing and face paint; it reveals the true nature of things. Do you want this kind of exposure? It sounds inviting, but what would happen if the information you told a friend was leaked? What happens when you feel betrayed or backstabbed by someone close? Or what happens when you fail a friend? Pertinent to the areas of betrayal and loss are magnanimity and forgiveness. In the next few paragraphs, think of magnanimity as the umbrella topic, or overarching idea, and forgiveness as the spokes sticking out to support it.

Magnanimous. What does this word mean? From the Greek, *magna* means large, and *animus* means soul.[5] As a personality type, magnanimous means having a largeness about how you see the world, embracing a wide view of things for people and projects. To be magnanimous means that you can overlook personality flaws in others. In a pure dictionary-type search regarding the word you might find nobility, generousness, or altruism. It means to be great in mind and heart and certainly the opposite of magnanimity is pettiness.

Why is being magnanimous important to candor? Because candor is a two-way street. We can't practice candor in one direction; candor is bidirectional. If we give it, we have to be ready to receive it. In order to have perfect candor, one must be able to give and receive candor simultaneously. And, in order to receive candor, especially from friends, the candor-giver is helped by magnanimity and forgiveness.

There are a lot of definitions of friendship. Some I like best describe a friend as being someone who tells you that your hair does not look right or alerts you to a wardrobe issue before you go into a meeting. These items indicate an intimacy usually reserved for close relationships. True friends are those you can tell your deepest secrets to without fear of reprisal. True friends see negative things in us and can freely share them with us, and this is where magnanimity comes in because it is unique in the human experience to receive criticism well.

Few people possess a level of graciousness whereby even criticisms are welcome; but of course nobody likes to be a punching bag. Remember the concept of who we want to exonerate—usually ourselves, not others. We must resist the desire to exonerate ourselves immediately after receiving a criticism and try to listen to what our challenger is saying.

Some tend to reject the notion that they are wrong with the first hint that the conversation isn't going their way, but remember what General Marshall said about General Pershing? "I have never seen a man who could listen to so much criticism . . . Yet he did not hold it against you for an instant!"[6]

We have had some political leaders with a high degree of magnanimity and some with a low degree of magnanimity. Interestingly, whoever the leader is, and regardless of party affiliation, the common belief is that the President of the United States, for example, must have magnanimity. Perhaps it's because in that role, the President will be speaking to foreign leaders and other high-level members of government, and those conversations require diplomacy. Therefore, a government leader without magnanimity would hardly seem qualified for the job.

My take is a little different, however. Magnanimity is rare and may be hidden, until certain situations call for it. We only take notice of it when it appears to be missing. No one knows whether or not you have it until it is tested. Likewise, our close friends will probably only recognize whether or not we have magnanimity when it is lacking, like if we get offended at something petty and small. So is there a way to build magnanimity into our lives to deepen us and make us better people?

This goes back to the concept of love and treating others how we wish to be treated. To speak with candor to friends is to enter into the world of *agape*—the Greek word for love that means to love the unlovable, to forgive the unforgiveable, to give without expecting something in return, and to hear critical comments spoken about us without having to minimize or discredit the person saying them. It is about largeness in personality and character, not littleness.

How does magnanimity work and how can candor help? It is a twofold process: working on developing ourselves and responding to situations with others.

The first step is intentionally working on developing ourselves. Those pursuing magnanimity *want* to become better people, so they seek out negative things about their personality. They enlarge their self-awareness, and self-candor and being real with good friends is the way to do this.

You can practice this right now with a good friend. Think of the first two questions from the beginning of this chapter.

1. What is my greatest flaw?
2. What is something I do that really gets on your nerves?

Being a person with magnanimity means that it does not matter what the answers to these questions are, even if—especially if—you do not think they truly apply to you. Largeness, generousness, benevolence. These items are the appropriate response. Try this exercise with a close friend and see how it works.

In a contentious relationship, being a magnanimous person could mean a couple of things: that you can disagree with someone without demonizing them, and that you can learn from critical people knowing there is probably some truth to what they are saying. Charles Spurgeon once said, "Get a friend to tell you your faults, or better still, welcome an enemy who will watch you keenly and sting you savagely. What a blessing such an irritating critic will be to a wise man, what an intolerable nuisance to a fool!"[7]

The second step of the process is in our response to other people. This is where forgiveness comes in. When someone unintentionally hurts us, the appropriate response is to forgive them. When someone intentionally harms us or a loved one, it is much harder to forgive. At some point in our quest to bring candor to conversations, we might receive criticism that to us seems intentional. Perhaps it was done in public and embarrassed us, or perhaps it brought to light something that was spoken in confidence. Or perhaps we asked a friend to provide us with some feedback, and they went much further than we thought they should have. Some of the criticisms were perhaps not justified. Some may unveil a critical nature in the giver. In all these scenarios, forgiveness is critical.

There is a lot of talk about the therapeutic effect of forgiveness, but this is not the way I see it. Forgiveness is not done to help us sleep better at night. While we can experience a therapeutic effect by extending forgiveness, it should be given freely and out of kindness for others instead of for our own benefit. Eventually, a person who gives and receives candor will receive information that could cause some heart-wrenching reflection. Magnanimity deals with the moment and the relationship. Forgiveness deals with the time immediately following the moment and beyond, and it deals with the inner reaches of the heart. When fairly or unfairly wounded, we can immediately forgive out of a wellspring of love for other people and because of our own character. What does it truly cost us when we forgive someone? What do we lose by it?

It does not cost us anything to forgive, but we do lose something. We lose the right to punish the other person and exact vengeance. We also lose the opportunity to see another person suffer for what they did to us. There are forces in us that desire these things. It may seem that God would not be just if those who oppose us do not end up suffering. Yet when we take these matters into our own hands, we experience even greater loss, not gain, and we definitely become less connected to the other person, not closer. Thus, forgiveness is the passage for us toward greater gain and closer relationships.

A book on candor would not be complete without addressing the topic of forgiveness because words can hurt, especially words that are forthright and honest. We may need to extend forgiveness to others, and we may need to ask for it ourselves. So what is this process of forgiveness, and how does one go about it? Here are ten steps to consider when we need to ask for forgiveness or extend it to another person:

When we have wronged another person

1. Completely own the wrong in your mind.
2. State the offense to the other person without minimalizing, and say that you are sorry. Genuinely apologize and own the fact that you have hurt the other person.
3. Ask for forgiveness.
4. Discuss what behaviors you will change so that the offense will not happen again.
5. Reaffirm your love and support for the other person.

When another person has wronged us

1. Do not seek revenge.
2. Forgive the other person fully and, if the opportunity presents itself, do so verbally.
3. Seek to understand the other person.
4. Let go of bitterness and resentment by choosing to love the other person.
5. Be magnanimous to them in the future, having a largeness of heart.

Lastly, inherent in this discussion of forgiveness is a concept called unilateral forgiveness. We may not have an opportunity to speak to the other person. Perhaps they have moved away, or for some other reason we are no longer in communication with them. The charge to be a magnanimous friend and a forgiving friend may have to be done unilaterally, without the benefit of reconciliation; but we can still forgive another person and love them in our hearts.

UNLEASH THE POWER OF PRAISE
AND ENCOURAGMENT

Within friendship, there is an additional aspect of candor that deepens these relationships: providing approval with praise and encouragement. Friends have the unique opportunity to witness our ups and downs—when we're doing our best and when we are faking it, when we're moody or joyful, and when we stumble or succeed. This gives them ample opportunity to assess us and our behavior and know when to encourage us.

Everyone needs encouragement. Everyone needs approval once in a while. Friends with candor can provide this for us. Much of this chapter has focused on how friends can help us improve our faults. Another important aspect is how friends can fan the flames of our success. We don't necessarily need a cheering section and a trophy whenever we accomplish something, but it is nice to have a friend take notice of the positive aspect of our lives. Perhaps in the hard things or even in our disappointments, we acted chivalrously, or bravely, or took the high road when most might have chosen the low.

A good friend offers an objective point of view during those times and helps us acknowledge how we are actually doing. Remember the point that friends tell friends the truth? Well, friends tell us not only about our faults or character flaws; true friends are there to encourage us as well.

Here are three things to consider when giving and receiving approval and encouragement:

Speak up—When we see a positive thing our friend is doing, then we should speak up and tell them we notice, and that they are doing well. Perhaps it is a heavy burden they are carrying regarding one of their family members. You might say something like, "You are holding up so well in this situation. You inspire me to be more patient and forgiving in the situation I am going through." It is not hard to do this and it costs us nothing, but it could mean the world to your friend who may feel as if they are carrying the entire world on their shoulders. Praise and encouragement go a long way in helping someone deal with a difficult situation. Some people never hear an encouraging word. Speak up.

Speak often—It does not matter if you gave your friend a compliment the last time you spoke; if you notice something new to praise, compliment them. There is no limit or quota on approval. Obviously, this has to be done sincerely and with some thoughtfulness. But just because you said something nice yesterday doesn't mean you refrain from saying something encouraging for the next three days. Speak often.

Receive well—For many folks, it is easier to offer praise and encouragement than it is to receive it. I am one of those people. As part of my temperament, I do not like the spotlight put on me, yet I love to give encouragement to other people. It is important to encourage others, and it is equally important to allow others to encourage you. Be gracious about it. I have learned to bite my lip and resist comments like, "Ah, you're just saying that," or to think to myself that they don't really mean it. This may even be a form of false humility. Let other people be a friend to you and encourage you. Let other people approve of you without argument. As important as it is for us to encourage others, it is equally important to allow others to encourage us.

SUMMARY

In the actual words themselves, a "true friend" holds the concept of honesty. Having a true friend is to be in a relationship with someone who will speak candor to you and provide you an objective point of view. A friendship takes place when this behavior is reciprocated. Being magnanimous, loving, and forgiving are all parts of true friendships built on candor. People can take their friendships to a deeper level by speaking encouragement to one another, often, and receiving it well. True friends are gifts to us to help us navigate the world a lot better than we could on our own.

Strategy for Friendship

Right wrongs. Use candor with forgiveness and take ownership of the situation regardless of who is to blame. Don't be a victim, but think deeply about how you might have contributed to the disagreement; own it and bring it to the other person.

Reflection Questions

1. Do you have some true friends who you share candor with? Who are they?

2. What makes these friends different from surface friendships?

3. Do you have one person in your life who you can share *everything* with?

4. What is your own definition of magnanimity? To what degree do you display it?

CANDOR COMMITMENT

I commit to developing friendships where others can tell me anything, doing the same for them, being magnanimous, and capitalizing on opportunities to use candor to praise and encourage people around me!

CHAPTER 7

CANDOR with DIFFICULT PEOPLE

You have enemies? Good. That means you've stood up for something, sometime in your life.[1]

—UNKNOWN

One day a friend of mine heard a scream from his chicken coop where his wife was gathering eggs. No dead bodies were discovered, but his wife did find a black rat snake in one of the nests. When they pulled the intruder from the coop, they noticed the telltale signs of its mischief—a big bulge in its stomach. All the little chicks were present and accounted for, so the snake had obviously swallowed an egg. But they did not understand why an easily-breakable egg was still causing such a bulge in its stomach.

They scanned the chicken coop again and realized that one of the ceramic dummy eggs was missing. The snake had no doubt swallowed one. Farmers use dummy eggs as an effective tool to show chickens where to lay, otherwise the chickens lay their eggs just about anywhere. The snake had swallowed something that would never satisfy its hunger and instead condemned it to an agonizing death. Snakes cannot crush, digest, or regurgitate ceramic eggs, nor can they eat anything else while it remains lodged in their body.

Luckily for this snake, my friend's son came to the rescue. After some web research on how to dislodge such obstructions, he gently massaged the lump back up the snake's throat and out its mouth. Though this was certainly unpleasant for the snake, it saved its life.[2]

Candor with difficult people can sometimes feel like that for the recipient—extremely unpleasant. In the moment, if you are using forthright honesty, they may not believe you are actually trying to help them. But in the long run you are.

It can seem like some people have been put on this earth just to annoy others. I call these folks "growth people" for two reasons. The first is that they challenge me to grow in patience, and the second is that they need to grow a little bit as well, perhaps in self-awareness.

There is a distinction between difficult people and those people around us with whom we disagree. I disagree with my family members and extended family and friends periodically, but I would not call them difficult people. I am sure that occasionally I have been the one who caused difficulty in my close relationships. All relationships endure hard times. Usually an increase in understanding, listening, and love shown at key moments helps resolve conflicts and disagreements.

However, I define difficult people as those who seem to have no desire for close relationships and are content with stirring the pot and hurting others' feelings. These people willfully say things that can be harmful to others. They are not guided by the usual norms of courtesy and respect. Remember the situation I described in the leadership chapter about my supervisor who tapped my chest? He would use societal candor to remind me I was just a major, and if I did not change, he would ruin my career.

Understanding the various types of difficult people can aid in identifying when to make a bold move and approach a situation with true candor. The four different types of difficult people I have identified include: Roosters, Termites, Wolves, and Curmudgeons.

FOUR TYPES OF DIFFICULT PEOPLE

Hawaii has a chicken problem. The story goes that decades ago a couple hurricanes shattered coops and sent chickens flying all over the island.[3] Now, chickens roam wild, especially at state parks and empty lots. I relocated from Honolulu into a country residence on Oahu where there was an abandoned house just to the north. That is when my troubles began because it was the home of an annoying rooster. Every morning around 4 a.m., the penetrating rooster's crow invaded several houses in the neighborhood.

No one in the area has central air, so having the windows open is critical, and our undoing. One of my neighbors had been putting up with the rooster for months. Something had to be done. I soon developed a plan to catch him for relocation, but after a few attempts, he grew wise to my aim and expertly darted away at the first sign of my presence. It took weeks, but I finally trapped him.

This noisy neighbor serves as a perfect illustration for the first type of difficult people we'll discuss: the **Roosters**. These are people who are openly annoying. They say things to generate a response, either intentionally out of malice or with a lack of awareness to others' feelings, causing disruptions in everything from meetings to close relationships. These people sometimes go unchecked for years because we tend to avoid them instead of deal with them. Let's be real: roosters can annoy the heck out of you. They often say things to garner attention, unaware or uncaring as to how their actions affect others. Like the actual rooster who lived next door, the rooster-type can become wise to your purpose and avoid letting you speak, continuing to deliver their daily destructive communication to everyone around them.

Another type of difficult people is the **Termites**, secretly causing damage behind the scenes. They would be too ashamed to do so in the open. One of the hallmarks of termites is that they are known to spread gossip. In group settings, they can exhibit a kind of quiet resistance. For instance, rather than bring up issues for discussion during a meeting when something good could come out of it, they instead voice complaints among coworkers after the meeting. They may intentionally breed dissatisfaction in others as a way of influence. They are also known to be chameleons and will say one thing to you and then something different to someone else.

The third type is the **Wolves**, leaders who fail to lead and put down those around them. This type of difficult person could be compared to the Steward of Gondor, one of the most fascinating characters in *The Lord of the Rings* trilogy by J. R. R. Tolkien.[4] The steward was in a position of power and authority and used this position for bad instead of good. He could have prepared his army to battle the enemy, but instead sent others to their deaths in a direct assault against overwhelming numbers. He hurt those around him who wanted to perform well and was an impediment to progress until the very end of his life.

Sometimes the wrong people are placed into highly influential positions of leadership, and they negatively impact the entire mission and can even destroy those who are following them. Wolves are at the top of the food chain and can ruin other people because of their position. It's not so much that they smell blood and go for the jugular, however; they simply remain passive when good decisions could be made, and then go forward on the wrong things because they alone determined it was the right thing to do.

Last, there are the **Curmudgeons**. These folks are also perhaps known as wet blankets. They are resistant to change, put up road blocks to progress, and basically say no to anything new because it may be a threat to them somehow. They may not want to intentionally hurt people; instead, they may think they serve as the keepers of certain virtues they want the organization to hold. However, they tend to suck the life out of those who are trying to make changes and improve things. They are a little bit like the wolves in that they sometimes find their way into leadership, are generally very competent, and often have been with an organization or industry for a long time. They believe their duty is to maintain the status quo.

These behavior types do not encapsulate all of the difficult people we may work with, but these four types are examples of people who can greatly hinder organizational progress. Better understanding of these types of people (who may even feel like our enemies) can equip us to respond in love and work with them for the ultimate benefit of the organization.

A recruitment ad for the four types of difficult people might sound like this:

1. Disagree with everything, even if the decisions would be good for the organization.

2. Speak badly about your work associates, during meetings and behind their back.

3. Say nothing during a meeting, then complain about the decisions made in the meeting afterward.

4. Speak mostly about yourself and make remarks that may make you look better.

5. Monopolize the conversation, refuse to listen, and interrupt as much as possible to keep others with good ideas from having a chance to talk.

6. Talk about irrelevant items instead of issues that can affect positive results.

7. Make things personal, and take everything said as if it is a direct attack.

8. Threaten people.

9. Defend your turf at all costs.

10. Keep looking in the rearview mirror and talk about how things used to be, or how good the people were in times past as compared to now.

11. Speak for other people by giving anonymous advice to those in the room. For example, "Someone told me recently how much they didn't like . . . "

12. Don't ever let down your guard and enjoy the team environment. Don't ever laugh with those around you.

13. Think of yourself as an adversary to everyone else.

14. Allow for no negotiation or compromise.

Does anything in the list above remind you of someone you know? Is it possible that *you* may exhibit some of these characteristics once in a while? Since one of the topics of this book is self-awareness, take a moment to read through the list again carefully to see if you exhibit any of these traits. And for fun, try to pick out which type—Rooster, Termite, Wolf, Curmudgeon—each of the attributes describes. An answer key is in the endnotes.[5]

There is a tendency to reduce difficult people down to one bad personality trait, such as being prideful or self-centered, but this keeps the situation in a linear, one-dimensional view. With most difficult people, there is something deeper going on, due to nature (inherited and wired that way from birth) or nurture (acquired), that can manifest itself in various personality traits and many potential motivations.

Refer to the list again: Are the people displaying these traits exhibiting nature or nurture? Often it is some of both. There are probably a few who seem predisposed to being irritable or moody based on the personality they received at birth. However, nurture factors heavily, as people are influenced by life experiences, such as growing up in a dysfunctional home or being passed over for a well-earned promotion. Whatever the case, there is a nonadaptive way to deal with this type of person: we *want* to exhibit nonconformist behavior when around a difficult person for the good of everyone else who has to deal with him or her. The best way to deal with a difficult person is to respond with true candor. While our default may be to respond emotionally to their behavior, speaking the truth in love will benefit everyone.

CANDOR—THE SOLUTION

The good news is that candor, as defined in this book, is the perfect antidote to all these negative traits. Candor can be the sharpest, most effective tool in your toolbox in how to deal with difficult people. The initial diagram from chapter 1 depicts an increase of candor and an increase of love. Both are needed, and that is what is going to be so hard. Difficult people seem nearly impossible to love. But we should not use candor without its essential key, love. Difficult people have had the truth spoken to them a few times, no doubt, but not perhaps by someone who truly cares about them and has their best interest in mind. That is why the rest of this chapter can be an effective guide to dealing with difficult people.

First off, we've all been around difficult people. Sometimes it seems there are as many difficult people as there are congenial and cooperative people. But that is not true. Difficult people are typically in the minority and the good news is that difficult people can modify their behavior when honestly confronted by someone who cares about them. I have seen it work. The results are life changing. So how does one start? One must start with an honest, objective appraisal of the current situation. Who is the difficult person? What types of issues are they being difficult about? Most difficult people will manifest traits in one of the four personality profiles discussed: Rooster, Termite, Wolf, Curmudgeon.

One should also ask if it is necessary to make the difficult person's behavior an issue. We must avoid adapting to any form of toxic behavior, which can eventually cause a person to develop a type of codependence. For example, one person's bad behavior can influence others to such a degree that everyone else's needs are subjected to the will of the one. The continual acceptance of the difficult behavior reinforces it, which is the opposite of what is needed. Therefore, it is important to act.

Regardless of what type of profile they are exhibiting, the diagram below is a guide to help deal with them.

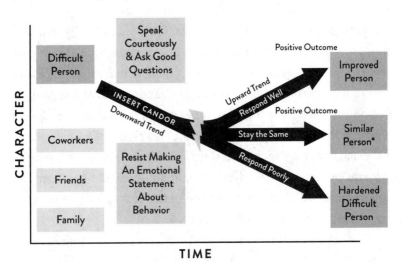

In the diagram above, we begin with a difficult person who, over time, will probably get worse if his or her behavior is left unchecked. This is where you come in. When candor is inserted into the situation, it sheds light on the difficult person's behavior and words; then, there is a real chance for positive change.

If the person responds well and engages you about the items you bring up, then you will have an improved person who grows with self-awareness. If the person keeps trucking down the same path, this is still a positive outcome for several reasons: the difficult person becomes more aware of his or her behavior in the future (thus the asterisk in the diagram), other people exposed to the exchange are encouraged to do the same thing in the future, and you are helped because of the milestone in courage and truth-telling. If the difficult person does not respond well and takes your candor as an affront, say, to their leadership style, then you could potentially end up with a hardened person who refuses to modify their behavior to help others.

Therefore, out of three potential outcomes, two of them produce positive results. There is only one in which the person remains on the downward path. What do you truly have to lose? They were likely headed there anyway. At the very least, in all of these situations, you have achieved something within yourself and within others for the greater good. It takes a tremendous amount of courage to ruffle the feathers of a power player, especially someone who has been left unchecked for a long time. You need to break the chain. Disallow that person to continue on the downward path. In essence, you are benefiting them, those around them, and ultimately the organization. But there are some important guidelines to consider before you engage a difficult person.

When you speak up about an issue, what are you actually going to say? First, consider how you say it. Speak courteously about the situation. Next, ask the difficult person questions instead of making emotional statements about their behavior. For instance, instead of telling the difficult person he or she is being rude or thoughtless, or saying, "You are being a jerk right now," ask one of the following questions:

1. Do you know how you are sounding right now?

2. Why would you say that right now?

3. Do you understand how your words are impacting others?

4. Do you want to clarify your remarks?

5. Is it your intent that your tone is so severe?

6. Why would you put it that way?

Let's play this out: Perhaps after you ask the first question, "Do you know how you are sounding right now?" their response might be, "No, please tell me how I am sounding." Then you have an opportunity to give them constructive feedback with professional courtesy. Such a statement might be: "The tone you are using right now can be taken the wrong way, like a personal attack, and though it may not be your intent, it could prevent some of us in the room from truly understanding or appreciating what you are trying to communicate." This type of approach will be far less damaging to the conversation than if you were to make a declaration such as, "You are being an inconsiderate jerk right now." The question approach exhibits love; an emotional statement approach exhibits frustration.

● ● ●

Our goal should not be trying to prove something with righteous indignation.

● ● ●

When faced with a difficult situation, our first inclination is usually to become angry or defensive. That reaction prompts us to make an emotional declaration in response to the person's unacceptable behavior. However, if we take a deep breath and think about the greater good for both the difficult person and everyone else in the room, it will help us to better ascertain an appropriate response. Our goal should not be trying to prove something with righteous indignation. Rather, it should be to help the situation by creating an atmosphere of respect for others, and it starts with us and how we approach the difficult person. It is okay to show some emotion; in fact, you probably can't help it because your heart will be pounding, but don't let emotions cause you to say something to intentionally hurt someone.

These types of situations happen both at work and at home. Here is another scenario: Let's say your question is, "Why would you say that right now?" This allows the difficult person to explain what they are thinking. Perhaps they are using some data that you have not been made aware of. Usually when they are challenged like this, their go-to answer is that it is the truth: "Why wouldn't I say this now. It is the truth, isn't it?" Perhaps they are using societal candor, not realizing it is diseased to the core and prideful. However they respond to your question, you might realize that their words are still hurtful to someone else in the room. The next thing to say is, "I understand that you believe these things, but do you also realize that what you are saying and the way you are saying it is not as productive as it could be?" This type of response might be more effective in a one-on-one setting.

Stepping up to the challenge of dealing with difficult people is, well, difficult. I asked an experienced farmer once what he thought one should do if there was a belligerent person in the room bossing everyone around. He said that, like a bull, you have to dehorn him. I asked, "How do you do that to a person?" And his simple response was, "It is bloody."

Not every difficult person needs to be "dehorned," and the ones who do should probably be confronted in a one-on-one setting. Most difficult people can be prodded with a little bit of true candor and will either improve their relationship skills or at least be circumspect about their behavior the next time.

In my illustration from chapter 1, I did not make an emotional statement to the chairman of the board. Instead, I simply stated that

I thought his name should be removed from the ballot. One of the cardinal rules of conversations is to speak for yourself. Never say things like, "I've been hearing talk," or "Someone told me they didn't like such and such." In fact, this particular chairman used to bring up anonymous issues like this at our board meetings, seeking to exert his will and influence.

• • •

One of the cardinal rules of conversations is to speak for yourself.

• • •

In my story, the chairman asked me why his name should not go up, and I took the chance to explain to him that I did not think the way he was leading was truly helping the organization. I mentioned that when a decision was made by the board, all the board members were expected to support it, even if they did not agree. When one member freely discusses conversations with non-board members, it makes for difficult situations. At the meeting, I said everything in a courteous, professional way. He did not agree with my assessment, but that was his prerogative.

Applying this situation to the previous diagram, at first it may appear that inserting candor into this situation may have hardened the chairman, but that was not the case. At the very least, candor made him more circumspect because he voluntarily withdrew his name from the ballot for the next year. At best (which was my hope for him), my candor improved his future encounters; and I saw some evidence of that before I moved from the area.

It's funny how when you run outside you barely recognize the wind until you face into it. A tailwind isn't as noticeable as a headwind. Think of candor not as a resistant headwind, but as a tailwind, gently steering a difficult person in the right direction, and in a way that is least disruptive and most helpful to that person and others. People who wield candor effectively in tough situations are negotiators and leaders. They exhibit courage and create more group intimacy by stepping into the muck and advocating for a better workplace environment, better business practice rules for employees, or even for a better relationship at home.

IN PUBLIC OR PRIVATE?

There are certain times when difficult people need to be confronted with candor while in a public setting. This is the case if the difficult person's behavior:

1. Is continually displayed in a group setting.

2. Has ramifications that affect the majority of the group.

3. Is purposely exhibited in a public setting to humiliate or disparage people within the group.

4. Demands a need for witnesses due to a complete breakdown of trust.

When all four items are present, then it is recommended to speak up in public. However, if there is any chance a conversation could take place in private, then I would recommend that as an alternative. The reason is that respect is much more easily demonstrated when there is not an audience. Defensive walls are not as high. Guards are not up. Confronting a difficult person in private is beneficial for several reasons:

1. It gives you the chance to think about what you are going to say and how you are going to say it. Emotions can run high for both parties in the heat of the moment, and you may make an emotional statement about the person's behavior that can be rude and not what you intended.

2. It allows for more discussion time. Usually meetings have an agenda and a set ending time. Bringing candor into a meeting could raise some good topics, but there may not be time to unpack everything as fully as in a private meeting.

3. It allows for more intimacy. I understand that intimacy is a word that is hard for some people, perhaps especially men, but that is one of the primary goals of candor—to create deeper intimacy, even with a belligerent boss, coworker, or family member. We may not often think of the word in that context, but one of the definitions of intimacy is to be marked by warm friendship.[6]

Our goal in conversations is not to escalate things in an effort to embarrass anyone. On the contrary, blessed are the meek[7] and the peacemakers.

HELPING THE DIFFICULT PERSON

At the beginning of this chapter, I shared a story about a snake who was thieving and destroying chicken nests. When the farmer's son discovered the snake had eaten a dummy egg and would soon die, he slid the ceramic egg down the snake's body until it came out its mouth, ultimately saving its life. When working with a difficult person, remember your role is to help them, not hurt them. The work you carry out in order to help might make them feel—like the snake—that you are causing more harm than good, and they may want nothing better than to disengage from you.

Candor helps in these difficult situations. Forthright honesty given in love at the appropriate time for the benefit of others is a needed corrective in our society. We cannot continue to sit in meetings with our screen-saver face on. We must speak up to help the difficult person and everyone else in the room. It is okay to show some emotion. Speaking to a difficult people is a challenge and can make one's voice quiver and hands fidget. When you have another person's best interests at heart, you can be passionate because you are not simply fighting for your own rights, but speaking up out of concern for this person and those around you.

This will take guts. But you can do it.

And the results could change the direction of an entire organization.

SUMMARY

Dealing with difficult people takes guts and maturity and is something most people avoid like the plague. There is a distinction between difficult people and those around us with whom we disagree. Difficult people frequently say things that are harmful to others, and the reasons may be unknown to us, though they are most likely a combination of inherited and acquired traits. This chapter breaks down four different types of difficult people: Roosters, Termites, Wolves, and Curmudgeons. Difficult people probably have had the truth spoken to them in the past, but not by someone who cares about them and has their best interest in mind. This is where you and candor come in. Asking tactful questions and avoiding emotional declarations will help shed light on the difficult person's behavior. Always remember one of the keys of candor is love and having *everyone's* best interest in mind, including the detractor.

Strategies for Difficult People

1. Start with where you agree, then explain where you disagree.
2. Always lead with humility. Assume there is information you do not know about the situation.
3. Work not for your own benefit, but for that of someone else or for the organization.

4. Avoid known trigger points, or points of contention. Button pushing is never an effective strategy.

5. When dealing with a difficult person, speak courteously about the situation at hand and ask them questions instead of making emotional statements about their behavior.

6. Resist the temptation to call someone a name, though at the time it may seem very fitting.

7. Don't question someone's integrity; it leaves them few options to respond. Question the thought process that led to their action and allow them to question their own integrity. Or ask, "Is this something a person of integrity would do?" Their own answer will be much more beneficial to them than your drawing conclusions for them. When you confront difficult people out of your emotions or attack another person's character, this builds up walls and diminishes their capacity to hear any other truth you may want to convey. Making a statement about their behavior is not as effective as asking a question about it.

Reflection Questions

1. Think of some people you have dealt with in the past who exhibit characteristics of one of the four difficult personality types: Rooster, Termite, Wolf, and Curmudgeon. Perhaps you can think of one person for each type. If you are discussing these questions in a group, explain to each other who these people were, what kind of damage they caused, and if anyone—including yourself—ever stood up to them.

2. Perhaps you are going through a tough situation right now at work or with a family member. Think about some of the solutions in this chapter regarding approaching the matter with candor and, tactfully, with questions. Is this possible to perform in a public setting or is the relationship too sensitive? Think about setting up a meeting one-on-one; would that make the person easier to approach?

3. You may be experiencing a tough situation right now, and the difficult person in your life feels like an enemy who is out to get you. What are you doing about it? If you feel like you cannot immediately apply the concepts in this chapter to the situation, reflect on the sections about magnanimity and forgiveness discussed in chapter 6. In what ways could that information and the candor tips in this chapter assist you as you seek to reconcile with this person?

CANDOR COMMITMENT

I commit to helping others by asking tough questions and not allowing others to be abused by difficult people. I will attack problems instead of personalities, and when I become aware that I unintentionally hurt someone, I will go to them privately to communicate care and restore trust.

CHAPTER 8

CHARM vs. CHARACTER

It's a deep and all but certain truth about narcissistic person-alities that to meet them is to love them, but to know them well is to find them unbearable. Confidence quickly curdles into arrogance; smarts turn to smugness, charm turns to smarm.[1]

—Jeffrey Kluger

In 1976, twenty-five-year-old Austrian Jack Unterweger was con-victed of the murder of eighteen-year-old Margaret Schäfer and re-ceived a life sentence.[2] The prosecuting attorney had an easy time of it. Not only did Unterweger already have a horrible reputation, with sixteen convictions, his own girlfriend testified against him because Margaret was her friend.

However, in prison Unterweger underwent an apparent trans-formation. He began writing poetry, then children's books, then a bestselling autobiography, which an Austrian motion picture direc-tor turned into a movie. Soon he became the toast of the Austrian literary luminaries. In fact, they were so convinced that Unterweger had been redeemed by art that they began to campaign for his release. Even two Nobel Prize winners, Elfriede Jelinek and Günter Grass, took up the call to free Unterweger because they felt his writing was extraordinary. To them, Unterweger displayed the soul of a true poet, a soul which was far too sensitive to be any threat to society.

So great was the support for Unterweger's release that, after serving only fifteen years of his life sentence, the penal system paroled him. On May 23, 1990, when Unterweger walked out of prison a free man, the governor declared, "We will never find a prisoner so well prepared for freedom."[3] Unterweger's autobiography began to be taught in schools, and his stories for children were performed on the radio. He became an immediate celebrity, appearing on TV shows and selling more books. In fact, he traveled to the US to write about the red-light district in Los Angeles.

But within the first year of his release, dead bodies of women began to show up in forests—all strangled with the same knot as Margaret Schäfer had been years before. As a paid employee for a public broadcast company, the former convict actually interviewed policemen and reported on these deaths. Eventually, law enforcement arrested Unterweger for eleven murders, though he was convicted of only nine of them. Some of the murders happened during his visit to the US.

Those members of the intelligentsia who had crusaded so fervently for Unterweger's release continued to support him right up to the end. They simply could not believe that someone so brilliant and talented was capable of such cruelty. And they could not imagine that they had somehow been duped.

Jack Unterweger did not live to serve his sentence. The night following his conviction, he committed suicide by hanging himself. Unterweger was brilliant, talented, and a monster.

Obviously, being the "best and brightest" says nothing about a person's character. And it was the intellectuals and artists who were deceived by Unterweger the most. Having a high IQ does not necessarily guarantee wisdom and common sense. Charm and charisma entice many good people. For some reason, the more important qualities of the human experience such as honesty, integrity, wisdom, and candor are not ingredients of success as the world defines success.

● ● ●

For some, it is more important to be seen as good rather than to actually be good.

● ● ●

This story is an extreme example of how charm can be used to deceive and destroy lives. Even so, charm over character in any situation can be harmful. In this final chapter, we will delve into using candor with character instead of charm, a critical distinction. We will also look at candor in the context of developing trust relationships.

For some, it is more important to be seen as good rather than to actually be good.

It becomes more expedient to receive credit for doing something rather than actually doing a good job. And we can become masters at being able to discuss attributes of character rather than truly living them. This is why apparently good people do bad things, routinely. We live in a culture of façade. Many have a veneer of honorability they can wear like a mask, when it suits them, to contribute to the magnificent self-portrait they want others to see and admire. Continual virtue signaling and false humility become second nature to them.

And it is not just the individuals who are to blame, it is leaders who fail to perform appropriate vetting before they advance certain people and promote them into leadership roles. Businesses are prone to these mistakes. In an article from *Harvard Business Review* titled "A Culture of Candor," the authors discuss why good people do bad things and conclude this:

It is horribly easy to create situations and systems in which good people cannot resist the temptation to do bad things . . .

ethical problems in organisations originate not with "a few bad apples" but with the "barrel makers"—the leaders who, wittingly or not, create and maintain the systems in which participants are encouraged to do wrong.[4]

Obviously, when leaders create environments where integrity is not encouraged, it does not exonerate people for not having any. Everyone stands or falls on their own decisions, words, and actions. Yet leaders must be held accountable for the type of climate they create. People respond according to the leadership they are given and when leaders are not ethical, it infects the people in their organizations. The same article suggested that, because of peer pressure, there was a "reluctance to speak truth to power."[5] They explained that in all groups, there is a tremendous desire to be liked and belong and be part of the "family," making the pressure to conform almost irresistible.[6]

We tend to think about the pressure to conform as being a middle school phenomenon. Remember how strong peer pressure can be in those formative years? People want to be liked and do what the popular kids are doing. When you substitute the popular kids with leaders, you end up with middle school 2.0 in the workplace, which lasts for the rest of people's lives. Instead of it being a stage people have to press through in their early years, it becomes a permanent reality. And people do not want to speak truth to power. Thus, charm, possessing a superficial ability to win friends and influence others, allows folks to operate somewhat successfully in this kind of environment and advance up the ranks.

What exactly is charm, and should you try to avoid it? Charm is the quality to attract something. It arouses in others an admiration for you and a desire to be drawn to you. In essence, it makes people like you. As it stands alone, it is not inherently a negative quality, except for the fact that it usually attracts others by externals. It is a superficial power of seduction. At its worst, it can be a destructive power.

Think of the charm of Jack Unterweger: he was able to pretend to be something he was not. He charmed nearly all the movers and shakers in Austria to believe that he was a changed man. However, after his death, when they really began to study his autobiography, they discovered that some of the stories about his life were lies. What had been heralded as great literature was later revealed to be colorful fiction.

One way to clearly see a thing is by introducing an opposite for contrast. Take character, for example, as a contrast to charm. There is no way to dupe anyone with it. You either have it or you don't. If someone is drawn to you because of your character, then they have identified in you real *you* qualities; qualities of the heart and will. Being drawn by these internal qualities will never disappoint because these qualities will not change.

Now, there might be an apparent problem with this argument because people were perhaps not drawn to Unterweger's charm in and of itself. It was his writing, his imagination, the way he carried himself during interviews that wooed them. But this actually serves to prove the point. People were allowing items besides the man's character to attract them.

What was the state of Unterweger's actual character when people were signing petitions for his release? He was in prison for the murder of a woman, and also had sixteen other convictions. These actions defined his life when he was a free man. Jack Unterweger was not a man of character and could not be trusted. Many psychologists have noted that a person's past actions are the best predictor for future behavior. Therefore, how is character proven? Over time.

Jack Unterweger was not judged over time, he was judged by his written works which *in time* turned out to be misleading at best, and lies at worst. The entire life of this man was a ruse set to snare an influential group of society to aid his release. It worked. Charm was indeed the problem with this serial killer. He used it to deceive.

People were brought in by an alluring mask. For Unterweger, it was more important to appear to be a changed man than to actually be a changed man. He discussed attributes of prison life and how it can reform a person, yet he wasn't truly being reformed.

Despite how extreme this example may seem, we have to be aware of deceptive tendencies in our own life. Many of us have this innate and intense desire to woo people or to have them like us, more so than having the desire to be a person of deep conviction and integrity—qualities that will no doubt eventually attract people.

So what does charm and character have to do with candor? The answer to this question is twofold and is vitally important to an understanding of what candor actually is and what it is not.

First, we must continually be on the offense against charm in ourselves. Because of a high absence of candor in many work settings and homes, when true candor is practiced and utilized efficiently, it becomes a skill and will set the person using it apart from others.

It is at this point when a seed of danger is planted. We might eventually become known for speaking our mind and changing the outcome of meetings. We might potentially be recognized as the one who stood up to the stubborn boss and brought good changes to the work environment. We may receive promotions due to our proficiency with candor. So what is wrong with these things?

When these positive practices are influenced by an intense desire to win over others' affections, i.e., using charm rather than being motivated by our integrity, it can lead to problems. Instead of making us double down on becoming a person of character, relying on charm can reinforce the idea that we truly are great, *self* is doing well, and we have innate abilities that can influence those around us.

This type of thinking takes the focus off others and puts it on ourselves. We begin to wing it. Soon we may find we are not the person of character that we've been presenting to others. Our audio may not match our video. Our talk is more impressive than our walk.

Second, as people of character and candor, we will encounter others with charm and very little character. We need to be prepared to deal with these folks who are not like us and do not operate under the same set of rules. (At the end of this chapter, I provide twelve steps of how to handle this type of person by leveraging candor and your own character.)

So what does it mean to have true character? Being true in character means our words match our deeds. The word integrity comes from integer, or whole, and when it comes to personality, it means there is congruence in a person's life; they are complete, intact, unbroken.[7] What you see is what you get. They are not one person on Friday night and another person on Sunday morning.

When candor is used by a person of character, it is like adding rocket fuel to the effectiveness and long-lasting positive influence that the person can have with others. Not based on charm, this effect has nothing to do with deceit or compromise. When a humble person of character speaks with candor, others are compelled to listen. The earth shakes, walls fall down, and that person is heard. Though you do not ask for it, people will admire you and be drawn to you, and it will not be because of your charm, it will be because your voice, like the voice of a lion, *must be heard.*

TRUST RELATIONSHIPS

Candor and character will lead you into a new series of relationships with other people of candor and character. These are known as trust relationships. They can happen quickly and they can grow deep very fast. It is the place where good decisions are made quickly, so it is important to learn about it.

First, it is important to define trust. Trust is having confidence in the credibility or reliability of someone or something.[8] Trust is earned by delivering on our promises and commitments. Therefore, a trust relationship is one in which both parties possess credibility and reliability, i.e., character instead of charm. Their credibility is evident to each other, and they are comfortable in providing forthright honesty. Then, a trust relationship can develop quickly.

These relationships are centered on trusting that the other person has your best interest in mind, and trusting that things of a sensitive nature can be kept in confidence. This is only possible between people of character. When dealing with people who do not have character, you cannot share sensitive information with them, and you are not able to form a trust relationship with them . . . at least not very quickly; and speed is important when trying to get things accomplished.

Jack Welch explained how this level of trust plays out in leadership:

> Leadership today is all about two words: it's all about truth and trust. You've got to have their back when they didn't hit it out of the park, you've got to have their back when they hit it out of the park.
>
> When they trust you, you'll get truth. And if you get truth, you get speed. If you get speed, you're going to act. That's how it works.[9]

According to Welch, where trust is built, there is truth in discussions and speed in decision-making. It saves time and things can get done quickly. In my story from chapter 1, once the board chairman was replaced, our trust increased and meetings became much shorter. A lack of trust slows down processes because of doubt, disengagement, and trying to decipher what people's words really mean. And a lack of truth is even worse!

What is the difference between truth and trust? Truth is the actual state of things, and trust is having confidence in the credibility of someone. Though two people can read a situation differently, there is an objective truth.[10] Truth also means no shading, or unvarnished. Spoken truth is a definition of candor.

Truth and trust work in tandem. When there is trust in the room, then truth follows. Good decisions are made. Candor is the bridge.

LEVERAGING CANDOR WITH CHARMERS

But what happens when you have to work with people you cannot form a trust relationship with? When dealing with people of charm and an absence of character, you are attempting to manage the unmanageable. They've embraced a lot of lies, and they become comfortable with them. They make it so you can only see what they want you to see. But they can't hide everything. You cannot assume any risk with these people the way you can with people of character. The goal is to use candor and somehow cut through the façade and get to the heart of the matter.

Here are some steps to take when having to confront a person high on charm but short on character:

1. Let the other person have the first try at defining the problem.

2. Exercise patience with every breath.

3. Express love to the person you are dealing with.

4. Allow your own rights to suffer before you act out of pride.

5. Speak what is true about current situation.

6. Right wrongs (yours and theirs).

7. Be transparent.

8. Clarify expectations.

9. Ask for a commitment.

10. Thank them for engaging with you.

11. Plan a follow-up meeting.

12. Hope for a good outcome.

Let's take a closer look at these twelve steps. The first step is effective in trying to get the other person talking. The first step is effective in trying to get the other person talking. There is obviously an issue. Sometimes when we let people talk first, we find out things they are dealing with that we might have never known otherwise. This strategy also helps to begin to build trust with them, especially if they truly feel heard. While they are speaking, you will be tempted to interrupt and correct, but it is important here to exercise patience and self-control. Breathe deeply and allow them to finish what they are saying. Remember the key to candor: when we speak up, it should be done with love for the other person. What does it mean to love? It sometimes means to allow your own rights to suffer before you speak out in pride.

Next comes candor on your part. Tell it like it is without sugarcoating. Right the wrongs they may be thinking about the situation. Let them know the truth of the situation. Also, if you have misread the situation or said something you shouldn't during the conversation, then this is the time to own it and ask for forgiveness. Issue an unconditional apology. During this time, it is important to be transparent, which is another word for being honest and free of pretense. But at its heart, transparency means letting them see your heart. This builds a bridge for the next step: clarifying expectations.

This is when you get to let them know how you are going to be counting on them in the future, and what will happen if they don't follow through. Ask them for a commitment. This will communicate the importance of the conversation, and in effect will form a contract between you. Thank them for engaging with you on the matter, schedule a follow-up meeting so there is already something on the calendar and you don't meet just when something is wrong. And then, walk away, hopeful for a good outcome.

It is important to start out with baby steps. After you ask someone who does not have a lot of character to make a commitment, you can either check up on them, which does not show a lot of trust, or let them have the ball and see how they run with it. Only the second option allows you to see if they can be trusted and meet your expectations. When they prove reliable with a small request, then trust them to do something bigger and better.

There is power in a promise kept. It basically does three things.

- It produces the fruit of the initial contract.
- It builds trust between the two parties.
- It gives a sense of accomplishment to the person who got the work done.

Build on that. Talk them through it. Explain how important it was to reach this milestone. Explain how it builds trust, and that you will be counting on them for bigger and better things. Allow them to enjoy the moment.

CHARM, CANDOR, AND SOCIAL MEDIA

If there is any area where charm especially creeps in with its attempt to influence the opinion of others, it is through social media. Writing and engaging others on social media platforms creates a chasm between words and corresponding actions, thus character. We can paint ourselves to be pretty much anyone we want others to see. Review the content in chapter 5 about the false self and creating a careful portrait of ourselves. Social media fuels this behavior.

Tweets and posts need to be kept short or people will not read them, so users get right to the point. But can people truly understand an issue you bring up with one or two sentences? I have witnessed people write seemingly innocent phrases such as, "My heart breaks after discovering what people truly think about _____ [insert controversial subject here]." This kind of sentence can create a firestorm of responses from both supporters and detractors, which can lead to relationships being torn apart. The chief problem is that readers are left with too many assumptions about the writer's current position, the writer's past activity regarding the statement, and if the writer actually cares anything about what he or she is writing about. Only close friends or immediate family members would be able to discern what's true.

Many people charm others with their social media presence. Don't be deceived. Look for traits of character that truly let you know who they are and if they should even be writing on a certain subject . . . and if you should pay attention to it. Too many of us rush into a debate only to quickly discover it is all fluff. Either the person who posted the inflammatory items did so to intentionally mislead others, posted items about which they do not care to know the facts, or posted items too soon before enough facts were brought to light. In all of this, however, there is something more fundamental going on—an underlying current—that the person writing is trying to paint themselves in a certain light, as overly wise or overly understanding of our times. Writing with candor here—it is almost comical sometimes.

It is enticing to charm others with social media so it becomes one of the great litmus tests to a person's character. Routinely, we discover how otherwise wonderful people get swept up into thinking they have a fan base, the attention provided by social media changing them to the point they begin to display narcissistic behavior. In the long run, it may be helpful to know what is happening inside of people, but it is also disappointing and heartbreaking to watch someone you might personally know go down this road. It's surprising how so many people's self-esteem relies on such attention each day, in order to keep the person feeling good about themselves. A healthy dose of candor with these friends can hopefully help raise their awareness and get them on the right track. None of us want to exhibit narcissistic behavior recognized only by others and not by ourselves.

Another troubling aspect of this digital age as it relates to candor is when people shut down communication without reason or without explaining themselves. This kind of passive-aggressive behavior is the antithesis of candor, yet is used frequently to communicate a message to others. When people don't respond to you, it leaves you few options, and unfortunately it can lead us to think the worst about others. We are left questioning why a person abruptly ceased to engage with us. In the dating world, this is called ghosting. In the professional world, there is no adequate term for how small this makes one feel and irritated at the person being silent. Please don't be that person. As a person of character, you can use candor and explain to someone why it is necessary to cut off communication for a while prior to actually doing so.

A final thought about social media and candor. It is easier to use candor from a distance, but what I am writing about is societal candor. In person, those who tend to be more reserved and polite sometimes become opinionated, prideful, and unloving on social media due to the false sense of safety the digital distance creates. They may not have to deal with the consequences in their personal lives, so they feel freer to put words out there carelessly; words they would never say to someone face-to-face. It is remarkable.

For people of character, it is imperative not to respond in kind. Let your words mean something. Let them be a reflection of your character. And may we all remember to never use social media to intentionally hurt another person or group of people.

* * *

I realize that a significant portion of this chapter is an assumption that we will find ourselves working with people who are high on charm and low on character. We need to know how to deal with these people without growing more discouraged each day. As mentioned earlier, there is another reason it is important to think about charm and character: to bring us back to the fundamentals about our own abilities, ease of working with others, and moral compass.

Unfortunately, it sometimes does not take a lot of money, fame, or power for some people to begin to change who they are and forget about some of the foundational character traits that got them to where they are today. There are stories in the papers all the time about people who have lost their way: newly elected politicians going back on campaign promises, businessmen committing insider-trading violations, and ministers living in the sins they preach against. What will keep you from losing your way?

Even the best and brightest of us can make huge mistakes in character appraisals because of people's charm. We need to be ever mindful that being a person of character takes time, and that only in the crucible of time and life experience can we best evaluate character, in ourselves and others. It is the long game that matters.

SUMMARY

For some of us, it is more important to be seen as good rather than to actually be good, and it is more expedient to receive the credit for a job well done more than working hard at the job. Charm enables people to be masters of deflection, whereby they can show off attributes of character rather than truly living them. Living and leading with charm rather than character is a trap some fall into, and it is usually just a matter of time before they are discovered as the fakes they truly are. We must fend off charm in ourselves, spot this type of behavior in others and learn how to navigate it with candor, and develop trust relationships that help expedite the accomplishment of good objectives.

Reflection Questions

1. Why is trust so important to relationships, and how does it speed up the accomplishment of organizational goals, processes, and deepening relationships?

2. Regarding the twelve steps used to deal with people of charm, which one of these would be the hardest for you to use and why?

3. How would you characterize your use of social media? Is there a tendency to charm others with it? Is it easier to utilize a good deal of candor when confronting others from a distance? How might you engage on these platforms differently after reading this chapter?

CANDOR COMMITMENT

I commit to being a person of character and using candor out of concern for others instead of using charm to uplift self. I will work carefully with those who need to grow in character in an effort to improve them and our environment.

The GIFT

There is a story of a rural preacher who had a multisite church. He would ride his horse from town to town on Sunday visiting three different communities. A ten-year-old lad who regularly attended one of the services decided that for Christmas he was going to whittle the pastor a wooden horse, like the one he rode to the boy's community.

The lad's mother watched him for hours working on the wooden horse trying to get it just right. Christmas Eve finally arrived, and the wooden horse was ready. The boy wrapped it up as nice as he could, put on his heavy coat, and then set out to walk to the pastor's house. It was a six-mile hike through the countryside, but the boy didn't mind because he kept thinking of the look on his pastor's face when he opened the gift.

The lad finally arrived at the house and knocked on the door. The pastor opened the door, and much to his surprise, he was met by a beaming boy who was holding out a gift to him. The pastor told him thank you and invited him in.

The pastor spoke to the boy and asked him if he had walked all that way by himself. Yes, the child replied. The pastor slowly unwrapped the unexpected gift. It was a wooden horse that looked a little bit like his own mare. Thank you, the pastor said, that must have taken you hours. The boy just smiled and looked up at the pastor. They chatted for a while, and then the boy put on his coat to leave.

"You're not going to walk all the way home, are you?" the pastor asked.

"Yes, sir."

"You can't. It's too far. I will give you a ride."

"Nope," declared the boy, "I don't mind walking back. I was expecting it."

"Absolutely not," said the pastor, "it is six miles and will take you nearly two hours. Let me hitch my buggy to my horse Butterscotch, and I will give you a ride."

The boy shook his head kind of seriously.

"Why not?" asked the pastor.

"Because. That's part of the gift!"

The boy flashed the pastor a toothy smile and ran out the door.[1]

Years ago, being especially honest with someone was considered a form of kindness. To speak to someone with candor was to give them a gift. It was actually considered loving to speak the truth to others. But things have changed. In these times, it is important to remember this: people are not the enemy. A lack of honesty, poor communication, and fear are the enemies of relationships and organizations. This calls for self-sacrifice and love.

In this book, I have challenged you to put yourself out there and provide this love to others without ever expecting anything in return. You may teach candor and model candor to others over and over again, and it may never catch on. You might have to keep going over it again with certain people, hoping one day they will understand and respond in kind.

This sacrifice that you embark on to provide candor by speaking up, with love, when needed, to benefit others . . . that's part of the gift.

The sacrifice itself is part of the gift. Knowing others may not appreciate your courageous candor, yet doing it anyway . . . that's part of the gift.

Understanding your candor might bring temporary disunity or hurt you professionally, yet doing it anyway . . . that's part of the gift.

Realizing your authentic honesty exposes the real you to people who may not handle the intimacy very well . . . that's part of the gift.

Grasping that though you are using candor respectfully, you might be treated with disrespect . . . it's all part of the gift.

Why are all of these things part of the gift? Because although candor is a benevolent act, it may not reap results. Speaking up is a risk and might cost you something, something you could potentially pay for . . . for a long a time. Yet you do it anyway, willingly, because you believe that where there is more truth, there is more growth, and where there is more growth, there is potential for more wholesome, life-sustaining relationships, which brings people greater joy. The essence of candor is that it is a gift; it is an offering; it is a passage.

In a final summation of this book, I can hear one last question from someone at the back of the room, "Why should I put myself out there like that knowing all the risks?" There is an answer for this in Scripture. In the first letter of John at the end of the New Testament, he gives us the reason, "We love, because He first loved us," and "there is no fear in love."[2] When we allow God's unconditional love to penetrate down into the roots of who we are, it compels us to love others; it is a force we are unable to restrain; it is a light that we cannot contain.

Thank you for reading this book through to the end. I am excited for the quest you are beginning, and I am hopeful as you go out and experiment with the candle of courageous candor that, wherever you are, more light will be shed, and our world will be changed, one encounter at a time.

Please share your personal candor stories with me at www.causeybooks.com. I would love to read them.

The 22 STRATEGIES for EFFECTIVE CANDOR

1. Speak to people in private, if possible, especially if the subject matter is sensitive in nature and can be brokered without a group discussion.

2. Make it a point to engage the difficult topics. This is counterintuitive and seems dangerous. However, sometimes you have to go out on a limb because that is where the fruit is.

3. Go for gold. Speak about the most important issue that needs to be addressed. Sometimes the smaller items evaporate when the bigger ones are dealt with.

4. Instead of focusing on risks, focus on results. We are sometimes overly afraid of negative outcomes.

5. Avoid the word "just." It shows weakness or, worse, a passive-aggressive nature. For instance, "If you could just redo that presentation for me to make it better . . ." Simply ask or tell someone to do something. Using the word *just* belies the task, making it

sound simple, even when you are asking something that might be challenging. Using the word *just* does not display candor.

6. Love others generously. Show the other person through your tone and facial expression that you care about him or her.

7. Resist the temptation to tell people simply what you think they want to hear. Tell others what they need to hear. Avoid the urge to be a people pleaser.

8. Don't be overly concerned about the impression you are making; try to find the most truthful and helpful points to the discussion.

9. Follow-up your candor when the meeting concludes. Your words may not have been taken in the way you meant them, or you may have said the wrong thing. Follow-up and readdress the issue as soon as possible when needed.

10. Attack the problem, not the personality. Give others the benefit of the doubt until they show all their cards. Communicate an abundance of trust until you are proven wrong.

11. Don't think "last laugh," think "win-win." How could demonstrating candor positively impact the situation and bring it to a good conclusion? Think in terms of positivity: what is the best case or most hopeful outcome?

12. When unable to reach a conclusive decision, agree to readdress the topic later. A healthy pause might be more helpful to the relationship than a personal win.

13. Avoid superlatives, such as "you always," "I never," etc. These are seldom, if ever, true, so they do not qualify as candor.

14. For maximum impact, work through bad moods, and speak to the issue while it is on the table. This means your bad moods and

others' bad moods. It means we must be in the moment, listen attentively, and ask someone to repeat something that does not sound quite right. This will provide time to take a deep breath and think while others are talking.

15. Right wrongs. Use candor with forgiveness, and take ownership of the situation regarding who is to blame. Don't be a victim, but think deeply about how you might have contributed to the disagreement. Own it and bring it to the other person.

16. Start with where you agree, then explain where you disagree.

17. Always lead with humility. Assume there is information you do not know about the situation.

18. Work not for your own benefit, but for that of someone else or for the organization.

19. Avoid known trigger points or points of contention. Button pushing is never an effective strategy.

20. When dealing with a difficult person, speak courteously about the situation at hand and ask them questions instead of making emotional statements about their behavior.

21. Resist the temptation to call someone a name, though at the time it may seem very fitting.

22. Don't question someone's integrity; it leaves them few options to respond. Question the thought process that led to their actions, and allow them to question their own integrity. Or ask, "Is this something a person of integrity would do?" Their own answer will be much more beneficial to them than your drawing conclusions for them.

The EIGHT CANDOR COMMITMENTS

1. I commit to speaking the unspoken truth, with love, when needed, to benefit others!

2. I commit to identifying the enemies of candor in myself and defeating them with love and trust!

3. I am committed to my organization; therefore, I will give and receive candor when needed. I also commit to giving others the benefit of the doubt and resisting the temptation to tell others simply what I think they want to hear.

4. I commit to treating people in my family with dignity and respect. All of my relationships are important but especially those whom I am committed to love. I promise to speak to them with candor!

5. I commit to using candor with myself by asking tough questions, seeking honest answers, and being observant and reflective in regard to what others are saying about my behavior. Instead of wearing a mask, I want to be in touch with how I am really doing so I can be honest with myself and other people, and thus reach the goal of self-awareness.

6. I commit to developing friendships where others can tell me anything, doing the same for them, being magnanimous, and capitalizing on opportunities to use candor to praise and encourage people around me!

7. I commit to helping others by asking tough questions and not allowing others to be abused by difficult people. I will attack problems instead of personalities, and when I become aware that I unintentionally hurt someone, I will go to them privately to communicate care and restore trust.

8. I commit to being a person of character and using candor out of concern for others instead of using charm to uplift self. I will work carefully with those who need to grow in character in an effort to improve them and our environment.

DISCUSSION QUESTIONS for GROUPS

1. Is it easy for you to speak with candor? Why or why not?

2. In your own words, what is the difference between societal candor and true candor?

3. Have you seen much true candor in your lifetime?

4. Which enemy of candor impacts you the most? Explain.

5. Describe a situation where you displayed a fear or a lack of confidence in speaking up.

6. Have you ever experienced feeling misunderstood in the workplace like Anna from chapter 3? What did you do about it?

7. Recall the three types of leaders: Transactional, Trainwreck, and Transformative. Based on your understanding of this chapter, which type of leadership style have you displayed in the past? Do you sway more to the love category or to the candor category?

8. Do you regularly ask for feedback from your subordinates? Do you receive it appropriately?

9. How are your current listening skills? Do you believe that when you listen you are free to receive, to accept, or to reject based on what is being said?

10. Is it a challenge to be humble around your family members and truly listen to them? What about with your in-laws or parents?

11. In your own words, why do you think it is important not to automatically question someone's integrity?

12. Think of the chapter "Blistering Honesty with Self." What are some of the false masks that you wear?

13. Do you feel the need to routinely try to present to others the best scenario of your life as possible?

14. Think for a moment about your friendships. Do they display a high degree of candor? Give an example of a relationship you are in where there is a lot of candor, and one where there is not.

15. From chapter 6, what are the three quick ideas about encouragement and praise? Are you good at doing these things?

16. What are the four types of difficult people as outlined in chapter 7? Do you know anyone who fits one of these profiles? Explain.

17. Have you ever been in a tense situation where you had to use candor with someone who had a difficult personality? Explain.

18. What is your definition of charm? Have you ever met someone who had a lot of charm and deceived people because he or she did not have character? Explain.

19. In your own words, why is trust so important to relationships, and how does it speed up the accomplishment of organizational goals, processes, and deepening relationships?

20. What are your greatest takeaways from this book? How do you plan to implement them?

ACKNOWLEDGMENTS

Deepest and sincere thanks to Lauri, Nickolas, Madison, Hannah, and Isaiah, with whom the concepts of this book were forged. You have shown me abundant love, magnanimity, and forgiveness. I thank the Moody Publishers family for their support, encouragement, and all the hard work getting this manuscript ready. Their gracious offer to publish *Candor* came the week my father passed away.

There are friends of mine, too numerous to name here, who have been patient with me when I experienced a fear of candor, or displayed candor out of fear. I hold much gratitude for these enduring friendships. Many thanks go to those who contributed ideas and stories about candor along the way, including my siblings, Calvin, Carol, and Nathanael, and various other trusted advisors. I appreciate retired Army Chaplain David Causey who introduced me to some of the stories used in this book and kindly allowed me to re-tell them. I also appreciate all those who endorsed *Candor*, and those who allowed me an interview, including Dr. Gretchen Gee, who has been a true friend for over thirty years.

I am indebted to two pastors who have shown abundant support, Quintin Stieff and Tony Miltenberger. Quintin is a role model I look up to and a longtime friend of our extended family. Tony is a former chaplain assistant turned coauthor who has developed into a world-class podcast interviewer with his *Reclamation Podcast*. Thanks also to Alan Cole, who is my project collaborator and accountability partner.

When I think about candor in relationships, I am reminded of a dear older couple Lauri and I befriended when we were first married, Dale and Jeanne Quesenbury. They were ultra-honest with each other, and with us, to the degree that it was always refreshing and invigorating to spend time with them. I learned about some of my many flaws during visits to their home. At Jeanne's funeral, I explained that one always knew where one stood with Jeanne, and though you may not always like what she said, it was her unvarnished self being engaged with you, and loving you. I thank God for that precious couple and those poignant moments that pierced our hearts. They were instruments modeling for us the grit needed to be long-haul trusted companions.

NOTES

Introduction: The Emperor Has No Clothes

1. Personal interview with Dr. Gretchen Gee, January 2019.
2. James O'Toole and Warren Bennis, "A Culture of Candor," *Harvard Business Review*, June 2009.
3. Jack Welch with Suzy Welch, *Winning* (New York: HarperCollins, 2005), 25.
4. Hans Christian Andersen fairy tales are public domain. However, the above is a paraphrase of what is presented in Hans Christian Andersen, *The Emperor's New Clothes* (New York: First Anchor Books, 1983), 77–81.
5. "McCabe Fired for Lacking 'Candor,'" Merriam-Webster, March 17, 2018, https://www.merriam-webster.com/news-trend-watch/mccabe-fired-for-lacking-candor-20180317.

Chapter 1: Speak the Unspoken Truth

1. Ephesians 4:15.
2. Job 32:6–9.
3. *Merriam-Webster*, s.v. "candor," last updated December 9, 2020, https://www.merriam-webster.com/dictionary/candor; *Online Etymology Dictionary*, s.v. "candor (n.)," https://www.etymonline.com/word/candor.
4. *Cambridge Dictionary*, s.v. "candor," https://dictionary.cambridge.org/us/dictionary/english/candor.
5. Example is the story of Nathan and David from 2 Samuel 12:1–7.
6. Ephesians 4:15, 29.

Chapter 2: Enemies of Candor

1. First John 4:18.
2. Paraphrase of David Causey personal Facebook post, "Partakers of the Divine Nature," January 14, 2020, 8:36 a.m., https://www.facebook.com/david.causey.507. Used by permission. Source material for this content can be found in this article: Heather Murphy, "Man who had transplant finds out months later his DNA has changed to that of donor 5,000 miles away," *Independent*, Monday, December 9, 2019, https://www.independent.co.uk/news/world/americas/dna-bone-marrow-transplant-man-chimera-chris-long-forensic-science-police-a9238636.html.
3. As an army chaplain, I have gained confidence by meditating on what Scripture speaks about confidence in our relationship with God. Jeremiah 17:7–8 describes how the person whose confidence is in the Lord is like a strong tree beside a stream, fearing neither heat nor drought. Jeremiah 17:7 (BSB) states: "Blessed is the man who trusts in the LORD, whose confidence is in Him." Isaiah 32:17 explains that the fruit of righteousness is quiet confidence forever. These are powerful concepts for those who struggle with confidence.
4. First John 4:18.
5. First Corinthians 13.
6. This quote and subsequent thoughts in this paragraph are related to an article I read a while ago that unfortunately I could not find again. I thank this unknown author for their challenging ideas. It is very similar to ideas in this article, https://quoteinvestigator .com/2015/03/19/judge-others and similar to Stephen Covey's quote in his book *The Speed of Trust: The One Thing That Changes Everything* (New York: Free Press, 2005), 13: "We judge ourselves by our intentions and others by their behavior."

Chapter 3: Leaders and Meetings with Candor

1. Walt Whitman, *Leaves of Grass*, Preface to the Original Edition, 1855 (London: Trübner & Co., 1881), 22.
2. Ryder Kimball, "Jack Welch, the Former CEO of General Electric Who Grew the Company's Stock Price by 4,000%, Has Died at the Age of 84," Business Insider, March 2, 2020, https://www.businessinsider .com/jack-welch-the-former-ceo-of-general-electric-has-died-2020-3; Wikipedia, s.v. "Jack Welch," last edited December 5, 2020, https:// en.wikipedia.org/wiki/Jack_Welch.
3. Welch and Welch, *Winning*, 25.
4. This is a little bit of an inversion of the quote that is attributed to French philosopher Voltaire, https://en.wikipedia.org/wiki/Perfect_

is_the_enemy_of_good. In my definition, we are looking for the best but might be distracted with just good; whereas Voltaire is cautioning against perfectionism.

5. A climate survey is a questionnaire that goes out to all the office staff that asks about the work culture, and sometimes specifically how the leadership is doing. It provides a picture of the organization's needs and is used by the leadership to enter into a discussion with employees (perhaps at a town hall type meeting) about how to improve.

6. Stewart W. Husted, *George C. Marshall: Rubrics of Leadership* (Carlisle, PA: U.S. Army War College Foundation, Inc., 2006), 116–17.

Chapter 4: Candor in Families

1. Quoted in Joe Lonsdale, "Thoughts on Marcus Tullius Cicero," Cicero Foundation, https://www.ciceroinstitute.org/post/marcus-tullius-cicero.

2. I first published CAM with coauthor Tony Miltenberger in, *Unbreakable*, our book on marriage. I also wrote about CAM in my dissertation. Both were published in 2014.

3. I realize that for many couples the wife might leave for work early and the husband will stay home, or both may work from home.

4. Henri J. M. Nouwen, *Bread for the Journey: A Daybook of Wisdom and Faith* (New York: Harper One, 1997), 14.

5. C. S. Lewis, *The Four Loves* (New York: Harcourt Brace & Co., 1960), 42.

Chapter 5: Blistering Honesty with Self

1. The quote is from Jack Welch in his interview at GLS with Bill Hybels, quoted in Lillian Kwon, "Willow Creek Interviews TOMS Founder, Former GE CEO," *Christian Post*, August 7, 2010, https://www.christianpost.com/news/willow-creek-interviews-toms-founder-former-ge-ceo.html.

2. Temperament sorters that work with the Myers-Briggs Type Indicator such as the Keirsey Temperament Sorter.

3. This can be found at www.causeybooks.com or https://survey.sogosurvey.com/survey.aspx?k=RSsQQVWVUsSsPsPsP&lang=0&data=.

4. I understand that there are past experiences in people's lives that need to be dealt with in counseling. Here, I am focusing more on the one- or two-day seminar that is trying to help people. If they focus on either the past or the future in exclusion of how the brain is processing things right now, I believe it will achieve minimal results in the long run.

5. David G. Benner, *The Gift of Being Yourself: The Sacred Call to Self-Discovery* (Downers Grove, IL: InterVarsity, 2004), 69–70.

Chapter 6: The Indispensable Friendship Factor

1. Peggy Noonan, *What I Saw at the Revolution: A Political Life in the Reagan Era*, 20th anniversary edition (New York: Random House Trade Paperbacks, 2010), 218.

2. I believe that I heard this story for the first time in a seminary class on leadership in the Spring of 2003. The professor's name was Crawford Loritts.

3. Proverbs 27:17 (NIV).

4. Ecclesiastes 10:10 (BSB).

5. *Merriam-Webster*, s.v. "magnanimous," last updated December 1, 2020, https://www.merriam-webster.com/dictionary/magnanimous.

6. Stewart W. Husted, *George C. Marshall: Rubrics of Leadership*, 116–17.

7. Marshall Shelley, *Well-Intentioned Dragons: Ministering to Problem People in the Church* (Minneapolis: Bethany House, 1985), 107.

Chapter 7: Candor with Difficult People

1. Quote often misattributed to Winston Churchill. Similar to a quote from Victor Hugo: "You have enemies? Why, it is the story of every man who has done a great deed or created a new idea" (*Things Seen* [New York: Harper & Brothers, 1887], 63).

2. Paraphrase of David Causey personal Facebook post, "Swallowing What Kills Us," June 4, 2020, 9:18 a.m., https://www.facebook.com/david.causey.507. Used by permission.

3. The other Hawaiian Islands have similar issues. See Kenneth Chang, "In Hawaii, Chickens Gone Wild," *The New York Times*, April 6, 2015, https://www.nytimes.com/2015/04/07/science/in-hawaii-chickens-gone-wild.html.

4. J. R. R. Tolkien, *The Return of the King: Being the Third Part of The Lord of the Rings* (New York: Ballantine Books, 1965), 159, 383.

5. 1. Curmudgeon, 2. Termite, 3. Termite, 4. Rooster, 5. Wolf, 6. Curmudgeon, 7. Wolf, 8. Wolf, 9. Wolf, 10. Curmudgeon, 11. Termite, 12. Curmudgeon, 13. Rooster, 14. Rooster and Wolf and Curmudgeon. (There is more than one right answer for several of these.)

6. *Merriam-Webster*, s.v. "intimate," November 10, 2020, https://www.merriam-webster.com/dictionary/intimate.

7. Meekness means "enduring injury with patience and without resentment" (*Merriam-Webster*, s.v. "meek," last updated November 15, 2020, https://www.merriam-webster.com/dictionary/meek).

Chapter 8: Charm vs. Character

1. Jeffrey Kluger, "Narcissists Know They're Obnoxious, but Love Themselves All the Same," *Time*, October 27, 2011, https://healthland.time

.com/2011/10/27/narcissists-know-theyre-obnoxious-but-love-them
selves-anyway/.

2. Paraphrase of David Causey personal Facebook post, "Charm vs. Character," January 4, 2019, 2:54 a.m., https://www.facebook.com/david.
causey.507. Used by permission. Source material for this story can
be found at these websites: Mark Oliver, "They Thought Killer-
Turned-Writer Jack Unterweger Was Reformed — Then He Started
Killing Again," ATI, January 1, 2019, https://allthatsinteresting.com/jack-
unterweger; Biography.com Editors, "Jack Unterweger Biography," Bi-
ography.com, July 17, 2020, https://www.biography.com/crime-figure/
jack-unterweger; and Adrian Bridge, "Murderer's 'Final Freedom': The
Bizarre Life of Jack Unterweger, Poet and Killer of Prostitutes, Ends at
His Own Hand," *Independent*, July 3, 1994, https://www.independent.
co.uk/news/world/murderers-final-freedom-the-bizarre-life-of-jack-
unterweger-poet-and-killer-of-prostitutes-ends-at-1417861.html.

3. Mark Oliver, "They Thought Killer-Turned-Writer Jack Unterweger
Was Reformed—Then He Started Killing Again," All That's Interesting,
January 1, 2019, https://allthatsinteresting.com/jack-unterweger.

4. James O'Toole and Warren Bennis, "Why Good People Do Bad
Things," *Business Today*, December 13, 2009.

5. Ibid.

6. Ibid.

7. Charles Causey, *Words and Deeds: Becoming a Man of Courageous Integrity* (Colorado Springs, CO: NavPress, 2018), 15.

8. *Merriam-Webster*, s.v. "trust," last updated November 11, 2020,
https://www.merriam-webster.com/dictionary/trust.

9. Daniel Roth, "Jack Welch Says Only Two Words Matter for Leaders Today: Truth and Trust," LinkedIn, April 21, 2015, https://www
.linkedin.com/pulse/truth-trust-crap-how-jack-welch-looks-leadership
-today-daniel-roth.

10. Causey, *Words and Deeds*, 17–19.

Epilogue: The Gift
1. Source unknown.

2. First John 4:18–19.

RECLAIM YOUR HEADSPACE AND FIND YOUR ONE TRUE VOICE

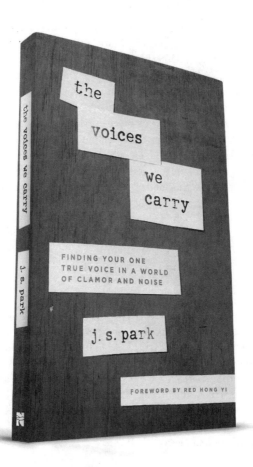

The Voices Model helps you find your one true voice. J. S. Park identifies the false voices we listen to as four inner and four outer voices. In *The Voices We Carry* you'll learn how to identify and silence these voices so you can grow fully and freely.

978-0-8024-1989-7 | also available as eBook and audiobook